SACRED PLACES

Sacred Places

British Columbia's
Early Churches

Barry Downs

DOUGLAS & McINTYRE · VANCOUVER

Frontispiece: THE CHURCH OF ST. PAUL, KITWANGA

Published by Douglas & McIntyre Ltd., 1615 Venables Street, Vancouver, British Columbia: ISBN 0-88894-285-0

Distributed in the United States of America by the University of Washington Press, Seattle, Washington: ISBN 0-295-95774-3

Publication of this book was assisted by a grant from the British Columbia Heritage Trust.

Canadian Cataloguing in Publication Data:

> *Downs, Barry,* 1930–
> *Sacred places*
>
> *Bibliography: p.*
> *Includes index.*
> ISBN 0-88894-285-0
>
> 1. *Church architecture – British Columbia.*
> 2. *Churches – British Columbia.*   3. *Decoration and ornament, Architectural – British Columbia.*
> I. *Title.*
>
> NA5246.B7D6   726'.5'09711   C80-091200-4

DESIGN: Robert Bringhurst Ltd.

TYPOGRAPHY: The Typeworks, Mayne Island

COLOUR SEPARATIONS: Herzig Somerville Limited

PRINTING: Herzig Somerville Limited

BINDING: T.H. Best Company

Printed & bound in Canada.

Contents

Acknowledgements

MANY THANKS ARE DUE TO THOSE WHO ASSISTED IN THE preparation of this book. In particular I would like to acknowledge the special contributions of Richard Archambault, Bill Birmingham, Father P.G. Collins, Ian Davidson, Henry Hawthorn, Beans Justice, Harold Kalman, Barbara McLennan, Julia Meadows, Rev. Raymond Murrin, Bernard Perreten, Alan Pierce, Juliet Pollard, Martin Segger, and Bill and Ken Shortreed. I am especially indebted to Susan Meek, who typed and edited the original manuscript, and to Robert Bringhurst, who so artistically refined the work and put it all together. Special thanks as well to Mary and Elizabeth Downs, who provided continuing support, and to my son Bill, who not only travelled with me but also printed most of the book's black and white photographs.

For most of the historical photographs, I am indebted to the Provincial Archives of British Columbia, and for several others to the Archives of the City of Vancouver, the British Columbia Provincial Museum, the Vancouver Public Library, and the Yukon Archives' M.L. Black Collection. Sources for these photographs are identified in the captions by their acronyms—PABC, ACV, BCPM, VPL, and YA.

My quotations from the letters of Father Florimond Gendre—in the chapter "Faith, Settlement and Church Building"—rely on translations made by the Oblate fathers and first published in Kay Cronin's *Cross in the Wilderness* (Mitchell Press, Vancouver, 1960).

BARRY DOWNS
June 1980

Introduction

THIS BOOK IS THE RESULT OF A FEW ROMANTIC NOTIONS I as an architect have about historic structures, their frailty and the interesting characters who put them together and used them. For over ten years I have enjoyed seeking out buildings that were part of the early development of British Columbia, delighting in their varied, often dramatic locations, and admiring the craftsmanship entailed in their construction. Early in the process I realized that, of the old buildings still remaining, it was the church—usually a social as well as religious centre—that best represented the cultural values of the period and that remained the best preserved in its original form. Houses of worship, after all, provided important physical and spiritual links with the homelands of the early pioneers and settlers, and allowed a continuity of belief and worship that was essential to survival in an untamed land.

My records of early churches encompass over a hundred years of building activity on Vancouver Island and the mainland of British Columbia. Several of our oldest churches still stand, though sometimes in altered form. The chapel of the now nearly vacant St. Ann's Academy in the city of Victoria was constructed by the Roman Catholics in 1859 as St. Andrew's Cathedral and was moved to its present location in 1886. St. Stephen's in West Saanich, built by the Anglicans in 1862, is Vancouver Island's oldest and some feel most beautiful church still standing on its original site. On the mainland, at Maple Ridge, can be found the restored but foreshortened Anglican Church of St. John the Divine, built at Derby across the Fraser River in 1859. About half of the original church was floated and hauled to its present site in 1882. Of greater interest perhaps are two superb examples of the English wooden Gothic churches of the 1860s—Christ Church at Hope, designed by the Royal Engineers and built in 1861, and St. John the Divine at Yale, constructed a year later. Both stand on their original sites and are actively used today as they were over a century ago.

Of the many churches and religious sites I have visited and photographed in the last ten years, over eighty are included in this book. Like others who have travelled similar routes, I was overwhelmed by the simple, sometimes primitive nature of the surviving handmade structures and the impact of a landscape which must be experienced for its vastness, ruggedness and majestic beauty.

I have generally avoided technical architectural terminology in talking about these structures, but on occasion there has seemed to be no substitute for the precise word, even for a flurry of precise words. All technical terms used in the book—bell cot, corbel, hammer beam, Tuscan style, and so on—are explained in the glossary on page 170.

Because in British Columbia the early period of development was the most vigorous and resourceful, I have dealt primarily with those years from the coming of the Spanish explorers, traders and missionaries in 1789 to the great religious activity of the 1880s. In the opening chapter I discuss briefly the religious architecture of our native peoples. I have omitted, however, the many railway churches, such as the famous stolen church of Donald, and the second wave of magnificent urban churches in Victoria and Vancouver, which must remain the subject of another book. A few structures from the early twentieth century are nevertheless included as well. I extended the book's time frame on these occasions in order to include particularly fine architectural specimens or to convey an important movement or trend. But my principal focus was the nineteenth century, and my intention has been to reveal the age and its master builders through the architectural styles and methods they used. Their legacy—these weathered artifacts constructed of available materials, situated to suit local terrain and climatic conditions, shaped to satisfy old and new spiritual needs—has, I believe, great historical and cultural significance. All the survivors—of which there are few enough already—deserve recognition and preservation before, as a result of disuse or neglect, they are lost forever.

Those Here Before

Labels on map:

Tlingit

Athapaskan (Déné)

Skine

Peace

Tsimshian

Kitwancool •

Wass

Skeena

Masset •

Haida

Skedans •

Bella
Coola

Kwakiutl

Fraser

Thompson

Columbia

Gwayasdums •

Salish

Kootenay

Nootka

© 1980 ROBERT BRINGHURST LTD.

Preceding pages: EAGLE MORTUARY POLE & FALLEN LONGHOUSE TIMBERS AT SKEDANS;
BELLA COOLA DANCERS AT BERLIN, 1885 (PHOTO BY CARL GUNTHER: BCPM)

WEST OF THE CANADIAN ROCKIES LIES A RUGGED AND beautiful land, rich in plant and animal life, yet in large part inhospitable to man. Its first people sought the beaches, tidal rivers and archipelagoes of the coast, drawn by abundant sea life and also by the mild climate, the gift of the warm Japan current. Here a complex and unique culture developed which drew its principal food from the sea and for its shelter harvested the land's greatest treasure—wood.

Salmon, herring, cod, halibut, eulachon and the great grey whale were taken from the waters. Salmonberries, huckleberries, blackberries, and numerous roots and bulbs could be found in the rain forest; birds and land animals too could be hunted at will. The magnificent cedar tree provided material for clothing, baskets, boxes, canoes, monumental totem poles, and for the timbers and planks of communal houses.

In this land of seasonal plenty, there were long periods of leisure, and the native cultures flourished. Complex societal structures evolved in which hereditary rank, lineage and possessions determined social status. Heraldic crests—symbolic representations of animals and supernatural beings—were among the goods which could be given and bequeathed, as were territorial rights to fishing grounds, berry patches and hunting areas. Songs too were heritable possessions, and extensive oral literatures of legend and myth were maintained. Deities and spirits of sky, sea and sun were worshipped, and the spirits of fish and animals were venerated both before and after the hunt. The ethnologist Franz Boas records, for instance, this prayer to a school of salmon:

O swimmers, this is the dream given by you, to be the way of my late grandfathers when they first caught you at your play. I do not club you twice, for I do not wish to club to death your souls so that you may go home to the place where you come from, Supernatural Ones, you, givers of heavy weight.

Inland, close to the Rocky Mountains, the nomadic Kootenays idolized another great fish, Ya-woo-nik, the Deep Water Dweller, mentioned in many of the native legends which, again, Boas records. Spirits of the doe, frog, coyote and chicken hawk also were revered, and it was said that two lynx had become the sun and the moon.

Farther west and to the north the Sekani, Tahltan, Carrier and Chilcotin worshipped a Supreme Being who controlled the universe through the work of spirits both good and bad. Among these Déné tribes, as among the coastal cultures, it was the medicine man or shaman who maintained communication between the community and the spiritual powers controlling life and death.

The house of celebration and ritual was, first and foremost, the native dwelling itself. Among the coastal groups —the Haida, Tsimshian, Bella Coola, Kwakiutl and Coast Salish—important secular houses were transformed into spiritual places during the times of great celebration. For the Kwakiutl especially, these were spectacular occasions —spiritual dramas acted out by firelight, involving masked performers and sometimes marked by acts of ceremonial cannibalism. But all year long, the house had a special place in the universe, as the centre or middle space connecting the sky with that mystic zone below the earth and sea.

Other religious structures sheltered the spirits thought to aid in hunting and fishing, and there were mortuary houses which often contained whole families of the dead— their many grave boxes stacked one upon the other. Totem poles too were erected to commemorate or to contain the remains of the deceased.

Today, many of these practices have been abandoned, but in some villages of the West Coast, winter ceremonies and potlatches continue. New poles are being raised by modern-day master carvers, and among the native peoples there is a new awareness and concern for the rich heritage left by their ancestors—those here before.

On entering the house we were absolutely astonished at the vast area it enclosed. It contained a large square, boarded up close on all sides to the height of twenty feet, with planks of an uncommon breadth and length. Three enormous trees, rudely carved and painted, formed the rafters, which were supported at the ends and in the middle of gigantic images carved out of huge blocks of timber . . . . The trees that supported the roof were of a size which would render the mast of a first-rate man-of-war diminutive on a comparison with them: indeed our curiosity as well as our astonishment was on its utmost stretch when we considered the strength which must be necessary to raise these enormous beams to their present elevation; and how such strength could be found by a people wholly unacquainted with mechanic powers. The door by which we entered this extraordinary fabric was the mouth of one of these huge images, which, large as it may be supposed, was not disproportioned to the other features of this monstrous visage. We ascended by a few steps on the outside, and after passing this extraordinary kind of portal descended down the chin into the house, where we found new matter for astonishment in the number of men, women and children who composed the family of the chief. . . .

This description of a Nootkan house was recorded by Capt. John Meares, English trader and navigator, in 1788.

KWAKIUTL HOUSEFRAME (BCPM)

KWAKIUTL POLE, VANCOUVER
Following: ABANDONED HAIDA HOUSE (BCPM)

Like Capt. James Cook a few years earlier, Meares took note of the idols and carved images and realized that these communal dwellings served both as shelter and as religious place for their inhabitants.

Measuring 30 to 40 feet in width and up to 100 feet in length, the Nootkan house was supported by colossal timber posts and beams 3 to 4 feet in diameter. In size, plan and function, Nootkan dwellings were somewhat similar to those of the Kwakiutl, Bella Coola, Haida, Tsimshian and Tlingit to the north, but the Coast Salish dwellings differed considerably in style. Simple shed forms with lapped wall boards fastened to a framework of poles, these Salish shelters were the first "attached" houses of the North Pacific. They were rambling, segmented living quarters set end to end, sharing common walls and measuring up to 300 feet long. Equally but differently ingenious, the Nootka of Vancouver Island created demountable wall systems of large cedar boards, which they floated to and from winter and summer villages and fastened each season to a permanent support structure of logs.

If the Kwakiutl and Bella Coola dwellings were the most flamboyantly decorated, the Haida and Tlingit houses were the best constructed. Faced with the need to protect against strong winds and cold temperatures, these affluent and sophisticated northern cultures built solid, weatherproofed timber dwellings of the noblest proportions. Close-fitting wall and roof boards, carved decoration and fine wood joinery were everywhere to be found in the work of these master builders. Their cedar beams were sometimes 16 inches thick, 3 feet wide and 80 feet long, shaped to size with a stone or iron adze. Inside the house, a number of stepped floor levels surrounded a central fire pit. If the house were that of a chief, the walls and steps might be carved and painted with heraldic images. Sometimes a carved totem, on centre at the rear, marked the place of honour. This totem took on special significance at the time of winter ceremonials, when the secular dwelling became the spiritual centre of the village and of the Indian universe. At these times, the house was sacred—and indeed it retained that quality in some degree throughout the year.

Certain relationships and patterns link this architecture with the Indian view of the cosmos. The house and its axis recapitulated sea, river and forest, and at the same time the house held emblems of the underworld (the fire pit, depression or floor), middle world (the space contained between four walls), and upper world (the roof). Within the structure a social hierarchy prevailed, the chief seated centrally at the rear, with others of rank descending in order on either side. This honoured position was also recognized when religious ceremonies took place. During the cannibal dance—the most dramatic of the Kwakiutl winter dramas—the sacred axis and distinctive locations within the house formed part of the ritual. The entrance, the central fire, the elaborate rear screens, and the numerous levels and roof of the building were all ceremonially used.

Indian Agent William Halliday observed a dance by the Kwakiutl cannibal dancers, or *hamatsas*, in 1935:

This dance was done by four performers, each dressed in a white sheet. Their faces were concealed, and as they danced round the fire they extended and waved their arms alternately. Four songs were sung during this dance, but during the third song the hamatsas, who had hitherto been reasonably quiet, now made a great noise, and ran hither and thither through the building, blowing their weird whistles.

Above the noise in the room, a strange whistle, unlike the others, was heard outside, travelling quickly towards the building. Footsteps were heard running on the roof, while the same wild whistle continued. One board in the ceiling was lifted, and a head appeared in the opening and uttered at the same time a blood-curdling yell....

The old hamatsas down below ran for a strip of canvas, and held it above the ground, into which the new hamatsa dropped. He was dressed entirely in hemlock boughs tied around his person, but when he reached the ground, after uttering an unearthly scream and blowing his whistle, he ran towards the back of the building, shedding the boughs as he went, until when he reached the outdoors he was entirely naked.

The festivities dedicated to the cannibal spirit lasted for many days and nights. The dance cycles utilized stage effects and props which would equal any today—trap doors and tunnels for disappearing acts, carved puppets pulled along ropes from performer to performer, elaborate costumes and grotesque masks—all displayed in spectacular fashion in the flickering firelight.

Kwakiutl interior structures were generally massive and plain, with the exception of a few carved support posts and beam ends, but façades were often covered with painted emblems or carved relief figures. Two major mythological themes were most often represented—first, the struggle between Thunderbird and Whale; second, the two-headed serpent, Sisiutl. The great bird who caused thunder and rain was traditionally depicted carrying a whale or fish off to its snow-covered peak, an act which symbolized the union of the two worlds of sea and sky. Sisiutl, similar in many ways to the serpent image found in Mayan and Aztec architecture, might appear on a decorative cornice or on a lintel inside the house supporting a ridge beam or entrance way. Usually elongated, the Sisiutl often included a human image at its centre, recalling a similar design motif found on the shamans' carved bone "soul-catchers." On house fronts, these designs were powerful, painted abstractions heightening the spiritual experience of the inhabitants.

Nootka memorial art may in some ways have reached its

Kwakiutl housefront with Thunderbird and Sisiutl (PABC)

high point with the death of a later Chief Maquinna (or Moqwina) in 1902. His memorial, raised on a rock promontory, was a three-dimensional tour de force. A great thunderbird, splendid in wooden feathers and paint, was affixed to a pyramidal frame and hovered over an inverted canoe form. With a long cut for a mouth and a painted eye, the hull was transformed into the great whale which the chief and his villagers sought throughout their lives.

John Jewitt, who was captured in 1803 by the Moachat Nootka under Chief Maquinna, related that the Nootka used skulls and brush to build shrines in the form of men and supernatural beings. Maquinna was also known to have in his great house a prayer box which he used to ward off the storms that prevented his villagers from fishing and attending to their work. José Mariano Moziño, the Spanish naturalist who visited Nootka Sound with the explorer Bodega y Quadra in 1792, recorded the existence of such prayer boxes in the houses of Moachat chiefs. Moziño tells us that the chief prayed by standing inside the box, beating the wooden walls with his hands and shouting his prayers as loudly as possible.

Burial practices varied among the tribes of the Northwest Coast. The Tlingit cremated their dead, while the Bella Coola and Nootka utilized sea caves or suspended mortuary boxes in the branches of trees. To the south, the Salish set the flexed bodies of the deceased in cedar chests

and elevated the remains onto roofed platforms located in the forest or on sacred islands. Among the Kwakiutl, death necessitated song-filled wakes, and among the Haida, a mortuary potlatch followed the passing of a patriarch. A typical event is described by the Reverend Charles Harrison, who lived for forty years with the people of Masset Inlet, in the Queen Charlotte Islands.

When a chief was on the point of death all his goods were brought forth and placed around him so that he could see his wealth which must have looked rather ominous to the patient.

When the Shaman had come to the conclusion that the sick man would not recover the news was imparted to him, and he was urged not to fight against fate.... The coffin was sometimes made in his presence. When in extremis he was invested in his cotton shroud, beads were placed round his neck and spots of red paint daubed on each cheek and a black spot on his forehead, and a white cloth was ready at hand to cover his face. He was then considered in a fit condition to breathe his last....

When dead, the most valuable article he possessed was placed on his breast, and one chief had a large basin full of silver dollars placed on his chest, another had a large clock and an immense watch. The nephew who had to succeed the deceased chief stood by the corpse and was presented with blankets, dishes, beads, guns, canoes, prints, pottery, dogs, axes and sundry other articles, not, however, for his own benefit, but to be distributed to those who took part in the funeral ceremonies.

The day after the death, the corpse was placed on a trestle and covered with a white cloth, and his effects were placed around him. The time for mourning had now arrived, the old women of the clan, the witches and the friends and relations of the deceased assembled and began to groan, sigh and cry....

After they had wept for two or three hours, the greatest chief present called for silence, and the "wake" commenced. Tobacco and pipes were provided for everyone present and smoking commenced. During this stage of the proceedings the chiefs and friends, according to rank, extolled the virtues of the deceased, and tried to console his relatives....

Everything done during his past life passed under review, then they concluded by saying that his time had come, that the gods wanted him and he being a good man had obeyed. The howling and wailing began anew, and was kept up at intervals both day and night until the deceased was buried.

Now at Skedans, an abandoned Haida village one hundred miles south of Masset, old mortuary and memorial poles lean into their final years of decay. Before the

THE KWAKIUTL VILLAGE OF GWAYASDUMS, CIRCA 1900 & 1917 (PHOTOS BY C.F. NEWCOMBE: BCPM)

The praying room of Maquinna (VPL)

villagers moved to Skidegate, twenty-five miles away, Skedans could boast of over fifty finely carved monuments, resplendent with the crest figures of the prominent Eagle and Raven clans. Beaver, Cormorant, Dogfish and Grizzly Bear were among the emblems owned, each elucidated by legend or myth and each signifying certain privileges or rights of its owner.

Of the poles which the Haida erected, two types commemorated the dead. The memorial poles were carved at the base and had a clear or ringed shaft above. The mortuary poles, elaborately carved or fluted, were thinner at the base and hollowed out at the top to accept the remains of the deceased. Their elevated chambers were roofed with boards and faced with frontal planks supporting the carved crest of the interred. Remnants of fine examples still can be found among the thistle and spruce on the old Skedans site. Ravaged by time and weather, devoid of their contents and their facing boards, they nevertheless represent some of the best work of the period, the high style of Haida art.

Many native people believed in an afterlife, reached through rebirth on earth or in other worlds, and constructed not only poles but grave houses to contain or protect the ashes or body of the deceased for this event. Today, one of the last remaining rows of mortuary houses can be found at the old Tsimshian village of Kitwancool, sixteen miles north of the Skeena River on the historic eulachon "Grease Trail" to the Nass. Submerged in the fireweed overgrowing the cemeteries, and close to the fine poles that once faced the river, are the remains of burial structures displaying gabled, pyramidal and vaulted roofs. Conical masts and grave markers reminiscent of earlier house-post designs enrich the setting. In a village that was one of the last to accept Christian ways, these small frame constructions suggest a vigorous architectural past, when the stately houses and the great poles of the Wolf and Frog clans dominated the river of the Kitwancool.

BEAR MORTUARY POLE, SKEDANS

FLUTED MORTUARY POLE, SKEDANS

GRAVE HOUSE & MONUMENTS, KITWANCOOL

Traders & Missionaries

Fort Babine
Fort Kilmaurs
Pinchi
Fort St. James
Fort Alexandria
Fort Thompson
Friendly Cove
Fort Langley

Stikine
Nass
Skeena
Peace
Fraser
Thompson
Columbia

© 1980 ROBERT BRINGHURST LTD.

Preceding pages: FORT ST. JAMES;
INDIAN CHIEFS & MISSIONARIES AT FORT FRASER (PABC)

26

TWO HUNDRED AND THIRTY-TWO YEARS AFTER THE DIS-covery of Alta California by Juan Rodriguez Cabrillo in 1542, the government of New Spain initiated a series of expeditions from their naval station at San Blas (west of Guadalajara) to the Northwest Coast of North America. Fear of settlement and trade explorations below the Gulf of Alaska by Czarist Russia, and concern for sovereign rights to the land found by others to be so rich in sea otter pelts, led to the establishment of the first Spanish outpost north of Monterey and construction of the first chapel at Friendly Cove on Vancouver Island. Named Yuquot by the Indians, King George Sound by Captain Cook, San Lorenzo de Nutka by the Spanish, the large bay inside the rugged coastline was known as Friendly Cove by all who sought refuge in its protected harbour. In the heyday of coastal fur trade and scientific exploration — for both Spanish and English expeditions were charged with collecting botani-cal, ethnological and astronomical data — the Indian villagers of Yuquot witnessed the arrival of many vessels: English, French, Spanish, Portuguese, and the Boston ships from the East Coast of North America.

Commandant Don Esteban José Martínez erected the initial fort and buildings at Friendly Cove in 1789. He was accompanied by six priests who, with great pomp and cere-mony, took possession of the land and the Indian village in the name of His Most Mighty Illustrious and Catholic Majesty, Carlos III, King of Castile and León. Planting a large wooden cross at the edge of the sea, they sang, chanted and prayed for the salvation of the natives and held the first Mass. Abruptly, Martínez was called back to San Blas and a year later three vessels returned under a new commander, Lt. Francisco de Eliza. Besides undertaking scientific and ethnological studies, Eliza re-established the garrison and constructed over twenty log buildings, in-cluding a church and a priest's house, as well as a church-yard.

Spanish occupation of the cove lasted but five years. The priests soon realized the disadvantages of the isolated site and lack of cultivable land (for most of the immediate area was rock) and were discouraged by the disinterest shown by the Indians who, under Chief Maquinna, vacated the cove in the winter months for inland Tahsis. In all, although they intended to christianize and incorporate the natives of the region into their empire, only a handful of young converts were found, and these were eventually taken from the village to serve and work in Alta California. The remainder were left with little more than memories of hymn singing and the celebrations of Mass and Holy Days.

Captain Vancouver however arrived at Friendly Cove in 1792 to find a settlement two years old and more extensive than he had imagined. His chief botanist, Dr. Archibald Menzies, described the scene.

After dinner I accompanied Captain Vancouver with some of the Officers to pay our respects to Don Quadra, Gover-nor and Commandant of the Settlement. We found him on shore at a decent house two storey high, built of Planks with a Balcony in the front of the Upper Storey after the manner of the Spanish Houses. One end of the ground floor was occupied as a Guard Room, and the other as a Kitchen and Servants' Hall, while the Upper Storey was divided into small apartments and occupied by the Governor and his Officers, who were separated by a large Hall in the middle where they commonly dined. On our landing the Guard was turned out in honour to Captain Vancouver, and the Governor and his Officers received us at the door, and conducted us with great attention and civility up Stairs to the Great Hall....

After leaving the Governor's we took a walk round the place and found several other Houses erected here by the Spaniards as Barracks, Store Houses and an Hospital on the Site of the Old Village formerly occupied by Maquinna the Chief of the District and his Tribe; there were also several spots fenced in, well cropped with the different European Garden stuffs, which grew here very luxuriantly....

There was a well-stocked poultry yard, and Goats, Sheep and Black Cattle were feeding round the Village. Black-smiths were seen busily engaged in one place and Carpent-ers in another, so that the different occupations of Building and repairing Vessels and Houses were at once going for-ward. In short the Spaniards seem to go on here with greater activity and industry than we are led to believe of them at any of their other remote infant Settlements.

The Franciscan Father Magín Catalá spent over a year here as chaplain serving the garrison and working to con-vert the Indians. He was succeeded by Father Gomez, the last of the early missionaries at Nootka.

Little is known about their church building, priest's house and churchyard. Indian informants in discussions with Father Brabant remembered "two stout men, both bald headed," who kept the Sunday-house at the centre of the village. Here, in front of the church, the heavy-cloaked Franciscans and the villagers went to their knees and crossed themselves, partaking in the ritual of service.

The form and character of the Spanish settlement at Nootka are depicted in an etching based on a drawing by English artist H. Humphries. Illustrated are the infirmary and storehouse (**A**), the commandant's house (**B**), the house of the captain of the troops (**C**), the frigate repair shed (**D**), the confiscated temporary boat shed of English

The Spanish settlement at Friendly Cove in 1792, after a drawing by H. Humphries (VPL)

trader-adventurer Capt. John Meares (**E**), and what was probably the church (**X**), behind the timber bell-mount over the pathway from the sea.

In 1795 the Nootka Treaty was settled and the Spanish flag at the fortress of San Miguel lowered forever. After many years of hardship, relentless rain and scurvy, the garrison sailed south to Monterey and San Blas. Within months the Moachats had reoccupied their old village site and demolished the buildings. Churchyard coffins were unearthed for nails which were utilized for fishhooks, and soon only the foundations of the church, governor's house and the well remained. Friendly Cove became once more the land of the Nootka—but at the end of the following century, the village was again to experience the zeal of the Catholic mission to the New World.

The Belgian priest, Father A.J. Brabant, came to the

Northwest Coast in 1874 to find the Nootkan tribes living much as they had centuries before. Within a year, he had established the second Catholic mission among them, at Hesquiat, some seventeen miles south of Nootka Sound. From this post, for more than thirty years, he travelled the wind- and rain-swept coast from Clayoquot to Kyoquot, a mission district almost ninety miles in length. His first sermons were held in the village longhouses. He spoke at one chief's house containing twelve families, each with an open fire supplying heat and billowing smoke, and lamented, "How could I instruct these people in such a horrible place of filth and smoke?—not mentioning the noise made by the quarrelling of the women, the crying of children, the growling and fighting of dogs . . . and then the immodest bearing of the numerous inmates!"

To escape such predicaments, he began to build mission

houses and chapels of logs at a number of coastal villages, but it was not until 1889 that he was asked to preach and erect a sanctuary at Friendly Cove. He imported lumber and bricks from Victoria, employed three Indians as helpers, and did the carpentry work himself. By this means the Church of St. Michael was built at the north end of the bay on the very spot where, 101 years before, Capt. John Meares had built the sloop *North West America*—the first sailing ship on the Northwest Coast. Brabant probably designed the church himself, and he describes the results:

To build a wooden church with the material I had at my disposition would puzzle many an architect. . . . I made the Indians get cedar which we squared and used for sills, rafters and other necessary supports [from] a supply of cedar blocks. . . . I made shingles to be used as a covering for the roof. Outside the building is neat, but the inside has the appearance of a common barn.

The Church of St. Michael (1889) at Friendly Cove (PABC)

The second church constructed at Nootka burned in 1954. Among the wild blackberries there is still a concrete footing inscribed "1788 Meares," and close by, Brabant's mission house stands in ruins.

Freighters carrying lumber and pulp down the fjords from Tahsis and Gold River now pass by the historic harbour where the ships of Spain once anchored. At the edge of a long pebble beach facing the Pacific stands the Church of Pope Pius X, named in memory of the pontiff who in 1908 corresponded with the Nootka Indians. Inside, two stained-glass windows, presented by the Spanish government in 1957, commemorate the historic meeting at Nootka of Capt. George Vancouver and Commandant Bodega y Quadra, and depict Father Magín Catalá preaching to the natives.

While the Spanish were still at San Lorenzo de Nutka and Captain Vancouver was still charting the mainland coast, another British explorer arrived by a different route. In July of 1793, after a very difficult voyage by foot and canoe across the Rocky Mountains, Alexander Mackenzie arrived at what is now Bella Coola. Eight years later the North West Company, of which Mackenzie was a director, determined to open this rugged land to trade. For this purpose the company turned to Simon Fraser, who in 1808 descended the treacherous river which bears his name, and who gave to the area the name it bore for many years: New Caledonia.

In 1807 another North West Company trader, David Thompson, had built Kootenae House on the Columbia River near Lake Windermere, and over the next few years he explored the Columbia to the coast. The navigability of this river made it the chief avenue of trade into the interior, and gave special importance to the settlements on its lower reaches. When during the War of 1812 a British ship seized Astoria, at the mouth of the river, from the Americans, it was almost a wasted gesture. The North West Company, which by then had achieved control of the fur trade throughout the Columbia Basin, had already bought the place.

The British built trading posts and forts from Bear Lake, north of the Takla and Babine, above the 56th parallel, south to Fort Vancouver—now Vancouver, Washington. After the merger of the Hudson's Bay Company with the North West Company in 1821, all of the western slope north of California was governed by Dr. John McLoughlin, Chief Factor of the new and more vigorous H.B.C. For twenty years McLoughlin maintained peace with the Indians, discouraged rival traders and settlers, and held the District of Columbia and New Caledonia in the name of the British Empire.

The Anglican Reverend Herbert Beaver was the first chaplain appointed by the H.B.C. to serve its traders, clerks and labourers at Fort Vancouver. After eight frustrating years ministering to Catholic-born, French-speaking workers and their Indian wives, he left disillusioned, his post remaining vacant for a decade.

In the northern settlements, too, there was frequently no one to attend to the religious needs of the isolated company employees. At Fort St. James, the most important inland depot of New Caledonia, the chief factor and lay preacher, William McBean, held services but displayed, in the words of Father Adrien Morice, only "vague notions about the Diety and the primary precepts of the natural law, coupled with vain observances, the main burden of which was reduced to shouting and dancing." From 1834 to 1846, the Indian wife of Factor Peter Skene Ogden ministered to those at Fort St. James. In this period the first Catholic priests arrived on the mainland, and their coming heralded an unprecedented concern with the religious life of the native peoples in the interior of the province.

Travelling the brigade trail which linked the chain of northern forts to Fort Vancouver was a difficult task. Father Modeste Demers commented on the slow progress of the crowded caravans, the hot sun and dusty trails and the monotony and weariness of travel.

The first days ... a person feels a general uneasiness augmented by various inconveniences arising from the uncomfortable position he has to submit to while riding a horse already loaded with his chapel, his bedding, his household goods and even his cooking implements. There is no halting until camping time ..., then everything is prepared for the night ..., the inevitable meal of dried salmon is taken and the sun has disappeared below the horizon.

In ministering to the Indians, the priests relied heavily on the Catholic ladder, a kind of symbolic Bible, printed on a long length of paper or cloth. This picture chart described the important events of the scriptures, from the creation of the world to the founding of the Christian Church. It read from the bottom up and in later versions illustrated two paths — one leading to heaven, the other to hell. This remarkable document, later redesigned by the Protestants to suit their own purposes, remained in use until the end of the nineteenth century.

Conversion of the native peoples was rapid, and the pageantry and ritual well remembered, though the religious message was often soon forgotten. A number of primitive log churches were built, and though all have now disappeared or been replaced, their construction marked the beginnings of a new religious life in the rugged, undeveloped country.

On their first expeditions to New Caledonia, the Roman Catholic priests sought the aid and protection of the Hudson's Bay caravans travelling the old brigade routes. In 1841, after establishing a Catholic presence in Fort Vancouver, Father Demers undertook the first mission north, travelling with Peter Skene Ogden and his company voyageurs from the Okanagan to Fort St. James on Stuart Lake. En route, he baptized more than four hundred white and native children and presided over the construction of a rude church at Fort Alexandria — the first church in mainland British Columbia. Soon another chapel of his design was built at Williams Lake, with a white cross over one gable and a chimney and fireplace at the other. Skins

stretched over the window sashes served to keep out the cold until they were devoured one night by starving dogs. Father Demers constructed his own benches, tables and altar, and on the Day of Epiphany, 1842, in the cold of winter, he celebrated his first Mass in the little chapel.

The buildings of Fort Alexandria have now disappeared, the last structure taken down for firewood in 1915. A simple frame church — St. Paul's, built in 1906 — stands on the site of the old post and farm lands. Here the Chilcotin once traded, and the voyageurs, who travelled by canoe from Stuart Lake down the Fraser to this spot, loaded their horse trains and started on the two-month journey to Fort Kamloops, the mighty Columbia and Fort Vancouver.

Fort Kilmaurs and Fort Babine on Babine Lake were the most northerly trading and supply depots reached by the priests in the first years of the Catholic missions. Established in 1822, Old Fort, or Fort Kilmaurs, was an important fur collection centre and a fish gathering station for the Hudson's Bay Company. Fourteen years later, operations were moved to Hwo'tat, or Fort Babine, at the north end of the lake, close to the trail to Hazelton and the Skeena. Babine is still inhabited year round by people of the Carrier nation, but its white- and red-roofed company buildings are now abandoned. A 29' x 63' church, constructed in 1915, stands close to the site of its predecessor, built of hand-hewn logs in 1848. It sits nobly on high ground overlooking the village and the lake beyond. Both interior and exterior are clad entirely with metal sheets embossed with a quatrefoil pattern — a surface material which in those early days was thought to be fireproof.

Father John Nobili, s.j., who visited all of the missions north of Fort Vancouver in 1846, built the first church at Old Fort. It was destroyed in 1925 and rebuilt to match the original. A single tower and a flared Quebecois clocher dominate the facade. Whipsawn spruce logs, planed by hand and clad both sides with wooden siding, form the walls of a simple, almost primitive interior. Bright green and blue painted surfaces enrich the space. Framed Stations of the Cross hang from the walls, and a weathered barrel stove dominates the nave. Outside, the ground lies vacant where the fort once stood, but at the edge of the lake in the summer, smokehouses and timber lean-tos are still filled with red-fleshed salmon being dried for winter food.

The great explorer Simon Fraser built Fort St. James in 1806, one year after the construction of Fort McLeod at the western edge of the Rocky Mountains. In those challenging days, a palisade and corner bastions protected the post and the dozen-odd buildings were spread out over a number of acres. Today, south of the present Hudson's Bay Company store and its red-roofed predecessor, are five buildings dating from the 1880s. The warehouse and fish cache (where the company stored its yearly food supply) are of Red River frame construction, and there are dovetailed log buildings which housed the chief factor, the clerks in residence, and the dairy. Restored by Parks Canada, all sit weathered and stalwart at the edge of Stuart Lake, close to the old company cemetery. Here in the long grass can be found a number of unmarked wooden crosses and the grave of one of the important early chief factors, Peter Ogden. Another, even more famous, employee was James Douglas, who in later years was to become governor of the new colony of British Columbia.

Our Lady of Good Hope, located near Fort St. James, was the principal church of the great fur trading region known as New Caledonia. Before its construction, religious services were held in the trading post every Sunday by the officer in charge and, on the occasion of their visits, by the Oblate missionaries. All company employees, without regard to their religious preferences, were required to attend these services, which were carried out in the Anglican manner using the Church of England Book of Common Prayer.

After early visits by the Romanist missionaries, Fathers Demers and Nobili, two others, Father J.M. Le Jacq and Brother Georges Blanchet, erected a house and a log church at the edge of Stuart Lake and formed the Mission of Our Lady of Good Hope. Constructed in 1873, the log church, measuring 25' x 60', has now been covered with clapboard siding, and a new Gothic steeple has been added. It is said that the original timbers were cut on the opposite side of the lake and dragged three miles across the ice by the women of the village.

Inside the structure there are now modern pews (early congregations were so large that there was not room for seating), the inevitable wood burning stove, and walls lined with embossed sheets of galvanized iron. Confessional booths remain, and on bright days stained-glass windows cast multicoloured rays across a white painted interior. Behind the church lies the log workshop of Father Adrien-Gabriel Morice, one of the most celebrated missionaries of the western world and one who almost singlehandedly led his flock to heights of religious understanding rarely achieved.

Anthropologist, ethnologist, philosopher, cartographer, historian — Father Morice was all of these as well as a beloved priest serving the Carrier and the nomadic Sekani tribes of New Caledonia. For nineteen years he laboured at the mission of Our Lady of Good Hope, ministering to the Necoslie Band at Stuart Lake and to the Indians at fourteen other mission posts located in a great area extending from McLeod Lake at the edge of the Rocky Mountains to Fort George (now Prince George) on the Fraser, north to Hagwilget on the Bulkley River and to Takla and Bear Lake at the top of the interior plateau.

Father Morice was born in France at Mars-sur-Colmont in 1859, educated at Nancy in the Order of the Oblates of Mary Immaculate, and in 1880 travelled first to Victoria and then to St. Mary's Mission to serve until becoming a missionary two years later. After a brief stay at the Williams Lake mission, he left for Stuart Lake and promptly began a study of the native language. Within a year, he had compiled a syllabic dictionary and soon was printing religious pamphlets, a school primer and a monthly review on his own press with type specially cast in Montreal.

His Indians lived from the land, fishing for salmon in the autumn with weirs and traps set in the great spawning rivers, and in the winter hunting caribou and moose, black bear for meat and pelts, and even the lowly porcupine for the prized delicacy of its tail. Morice travelled by horseback, canoe, raft and dog team, depending on the time of year and the terrain to be covered. Often his bed was of pine boughs laid on frozen ground, and on many a journey his four dogs were fed while he ate little or nothing. On these trips, Father Morice was continually surveying and mapping the territory surrounding his missions, and his diaries record many of his experiences. One episode indicates the hazards he faced:

September 21: Thirteen fishes in our nets this morning. We did not expect so many. The weather is cold, the wind icy, though we are visibly receding from the vicinity of the mountains. Snow, which is constantly falling, hinders my amateur surveying, while my crew are tired and sigh after the Nechaco River, of which we guess that Morice and Le Jacq lakes must be the headwaters. At last we reach the end of the lake; we can now advance along its outlet without paddling too hard. But what is that deafening uproar which we hear?

"Get up, John, and see what the matter can be."

"Heavens! The river disappears.... To the shore, quick...."

We were on top of a fall in the river! Having hurriedly landed, we portage our impedimenta, as well as the canoe, and camp just below the fall, whose continuous roaring would help us sleep if fatigue was not enough to do as much. My men are sad and dejected. Not expecting such obstacles in their way, they imagine that we must be lost and that the stream on which we camp leads into the sea, despite the fact that my compass and the tracings of my field-book assure me that, from Cambie Lake to the spot we have reached, our itinerary has been in the form of a perfect horseshoe. We are now, therefore, making directly

Text continues on page 42

THE METAL-CLAD CHURCH AT FORT BABINE

CHURCH & VILLAGE, FORT KILMAURS
Following pages: THE CHURCH OF ST. PAUL, FORT ALEXANDRIA (PHOTO BY BERNARD PERRETEN)

HUDSON'S BAY COMPANY CEMETERY, FORT ST. JAMES

FORT KILMAURS CHURCH

ST. PAUL'S, FORT ALEXANDRIA (PHOTO BY BERNARD PERRETEN)

Following pages: OUR LADY OF GOOD HOPE, STUART LAKE, WITH FATHER MORICE'S WORKSHOP BEHIND THE CHURCH

for Fraser Lake, our point of departure where we have to return.

Father Morice's greatest works were completed in the little log workshop still standing behind his church on Stuart Lake. Here he often spent thirteen hours a day writing and printing, living on fried potatoes and a few slices of bacon. In this unheated cabin—for he refused to buy fuel—he wrote geographic and historic essays, anthropological books, and printed a 328-page prayer book containing the church doctrine, religious readings, and eighty hymns all of his own composition.

Morice was outspoken as well as prolific, however, and was relocated to Manitoba in 1904. Along the way, his

Passion play at St. Louis Mission, Kamloops, 1901 (PABC)

printing press was destroyed and his syllabic type lost on the Cariboo Road.

At Pinchi, fifteen miles north of Fort St. James, stands a small church erected by the villagers and blessed by Father Morice at the turn of the century. Its hewn log walls and hand-decorated interior are representative of the simple primitive structures erected by the Catholic Church for worship in a rugged heathen land. Today the Pinchi Church is well maintained and retains its prominent place in village life.

Another Demers church was located at Fort Thompson—an H.B.C. outpost established in 1812 on a bunch-grass bank at the junction of the North and South Thompson rivers, across from the present city of Kamloops. Here in 1845 Father Demers and his Indian followers built a log chapel on the Mission Flats, immediately to the west of the company's depot. It burned in 1879 and was replaced by a new church.

Father Jean-Marie Le Jeune, who later worked among the Indians of this area, encouraged them to build on their lands, often to his own architectural designs. In 1900 he undertook extensive renovations to the log church of St. Joseph on the Kamloops Reserve, facing the city from the north bank of the South Thompson River. Here at the turn of the century passion plays were held in the wide street fronting the church.

Behind the same church was the small room in which Father Le Jeune developed and printed his unique Chinook shorthand, which he used in his teachings and for his newspaper, the *Kamloops Wawa*. On its pages were found village and world news, lessons, religious instruction and the good priest's editorials, all of which were circulated at one stage to over three thousand readers.

On the lower Fraser River, the first Hudson's Bay post was built at Derby, two miles downstream from the site of present-day Fort Langley. Founded in 1827, it was abandoned twelve years later because of continual spring flooding. Soon afterward a new palisade, bastions, and fifteen buildings were erected at Langley. Here, in the fall of 1841, Father Demers arrived to the sound of company cannon fired in his honour. During his four-day mission, he ministered to French Canadian, Iroquois and Kanaka employees of the company and to more than three thousand natives who had travelled great distances to receive his blessing in the fields below the fort.

The old trading store, one of the last surviving structures, is now used as a museum and is a fine example of French Canadian carpentry.

In the 1860s, across the spit of the Fraser separating the fort from McMillan Island, the Quantlen Indians constructed their first church. It was replaced in 1902 by St. Martin's Church, a simple frame structure with altar and seats carved by villager August Sleeptime.

Below and west of the now restored log palisade of the fort lies the High Victorian Gothic Church of St. George, built by the Anglican parish at Langley in 1901. Although of late construction, it is in a style the gentlemen of the H.B.C. would have appreciated, with a grand bolted plank door, a high steep roof, prominent gable bracing on the exterior, and decorative pointed windows, arches and diagonal panelling inside. A number of stained-glass windows illuminate the nave, some of them art nouveau in style, and others, such as the Good Shepherd window over the sanctuary, more traditional in design and rich in gold, purple, moss greens and ruby reds. Next to the church, on land which was previously part of the old Hudson's Bay Company farm, lies the pioneer cemetery. Its few remaining graves and rock cairn stand as silent memorials to those who served and worked the land when the fort flourished as a major depot of the great trading company of the Northwest.

PINCHI CHAPEL, STUART LAKE

43

ST. MARTIN'S IN THE DISTANCE: THE VIEW FROM FORT LANGLEY

ST. MARTIN'S, MC MILLAN ISLAND

ST.GEORGE'S ANGLICAN, LANGLEY

46

Faith, Settlement
& Church Building

Comox •
French Creek •
Nanaimo •
Cowichan •
Esquimalt •
• New Westminster
• Saanich
Victoria

© 1980 ROBERT BRINGHURST LTD.

Preceding pages: THE CHURCH OF ST. MARY THE VIRGIN, SAPPERTON;
DEAN EDWARD CRIDGE IN HIS PULPIT, CHURCH OF OUR LORD, VICTORIA (PABC)

THE ESTABLISHMENT OF FORT VICTORIA IN 1843 AT WHAT was then called Comosack, on the southern end of Vancouver Island, signalled the beginning of the colonial period, both for the island itself and for the mainland of New Caledonia. Governor George Simpson of the Hudson's Bay Company, alarmed by increasing Americanization of the territory surrounding Fort Vancouver on the Columbia River, had recommended the establishment of a more northerly fort in order to strengthen Great Britain's claim to the entire Northwest, and Fort Victoria was the result. Finally, in June 1846, the hotly contested issue of American and British partition in the Oregon country was settled, and a line through the Strait of Juan de Fuca, the Gulf of Georgia and along the 49th parallel was designated the boundary. James Douglas, who was then Chief Factor of the entire H.B.C. Territory west of the Rocky Mountains, prepared to move the company's headquarters from Fort Vancouver to the more northerly outpost.

As part of this plan, Douglas directed surveys and explored alternative trade routes from Kamloops south, through the Cascade Mountains to Yale, Hope and Fort Langley. Fort Yale and Fort Hope were established soon thereafter. Although the new route over the snow-swept mountain passes and down the treacherous Coquihalla and Fraser rivers proved difficult, it served to channel trade through British territory and contributed to the formal colonization of Vancouver Island in 1849.

As the town of Victoria grew around the fort, land development and settlement extended to the outlying areas of Cedar Plains, Esquimalt, Craigflower, Colwood, Metchosin, Sooke and on up the island. The land was cultivated and planted, sawmills were built and farmhouses and barns of rough-sawn lumber erected. From the great black veins beneath the town of Nanaimo, coal was mined. Sail- and steam-driven merchant ships linked the settlements, travelling the coast moving livestock, goods, settlers and a zealous clergy.

When in 1851 James Douglas succeeded Vancouver Island's first governor, Richard Blanshard, there were some three hundred colonists living between Victoria and Sooke, with a surrounding native Indian population roughly estimated at seventeen thousand. Eight years later, with the discovery of gold, the town of Victoria swelled to over four thousand inhabitants. It was a time of unparalleled growth, and with the settlers, merchants and miners came the call for clergy of all denominations. In the early years, dedicated evangelists, while serving the Indian population as best they could, ministered to the men and women of strong faith who had tamed and developed the land and towns. Together, overcoming the difficulties of site and lack of materials, they built their places of worship in the accepted ecclesiastical styles of the day, creating miniature but often beautiful wood replicas of homeland structures. Many of these fine edifices have vanished; others, treasured and maintained, remain in constant use. All are a tribute to the pioneer builders of that challenging and heroic time.

Accompanying Chief Factor Douglas when he founded Victoria on 15 March 1843 was the Jesuit Missionary Jean-Baptiste Bolduc. Eighteen days later, the first Mass was celebrated in a rustic chapel whose walls were of fir branches with a boat's awning for a canopy. Crowds of Indians—Songhees, Clallams and Cowichans—joined Douglas and his men in the holy service.

Eight years later Rev. Modeste Demers, newly consecrated Bishop of Vancouver Island, arrived in Victoria. Since 1838 he had served as a missionary among the Indians of the mainland. In a letter to a friend, he described his new diocese:

Why were you not there to witness a spectacle which would have been so novel to you! You would have marvelled and perhaps been edified, at contemplating the Bishop of Vancouver Island kneeling on the trunk of an old tree which the waves had rolled ashore, and taking possession of that heathen land which the successor of Peter has entrusted to him! That ceremony could not take place in my cathedral and you guess why: the lumber which is to serve in its construction is still growing in the forest.

Build he did, however, aided by Fathers Ricard, Chirouse, Pandosy and Blanchet of the Oblates of Mary Immaculate, who had recently arrived from France under the sponsorship of Bishop de Mazenod of Marseilles. The young priests took vows of poverty, chastity and obedience, and were known by their dark robes and the large black and gold crucifixes worn around their necks. In 1855, Bishop Demers toured the east coast of the island with his "Blackrobes," impressing his converts, he said, by his "long hat and crooked staff." Catholicism became well established, and in 1857 the Oblates built a small house and church, St. Joseph's, to serve the British sailors at the naval base at Esquimalt. This post soon became the official residence of Rev. Louis-Joseph D'Herbomez, the vicar apostolic of all the Oblate missions on the Pacific. Cayuse and Yakima Indian uprisings in the Oregon country had prompted his move to Vancouver Island. From Esquimalt, D'Herbomez directed all the existing establishments south of the 49th parallel, as well as all those later founded on the island and on the mainland of British Columbia.

As Fort Victoria expanded and more of the surrounding lands were subdivided into large farm plots, pressure was brought to bear on the Hudson's Bay Company to provide both schools and houses of worship. Education and religious instruction went hand in hand, and the first chaplain to serve the fort, Rev. Robert J. Staines, was appropriately both schoolmaster and a clergyman of the Episcopal Church of England.

Staines led an unpopular and tempestuous life while in Victoria. He is described as "a man of frills" who, in the view of many, cared more for his piggery than for his parish. A typical school day under this rigorous master was "a day of terror" consisting of morning prayers and church services, followed by hours of memorizing the Collects, afternoon service, tea, evening prayers, dispensation of a candy each, and final dismissal to a bed of "hard boards, an Indian mat and a Hudson's Bay blanket."

Staines was replaced the next year by the last of the H.B.C. chaplains on the coast: Edward Cridge, a graduate of Cambridge, an experienced schoolmaster, and former curate of Christchurch, Stratford, London. Cridge was a kindly but pugnacious man who was fond of the evangelical more than the conservative, ritualistic approach to liturgical practice. This penchant was to lead to a major upheaval in the Anglican Church in British Columbia a few years later.

Cridge, like Staines, having no church to preach in, held rudimentary services in the fort, on board visiting ships at Esquimalt, and at the schoolhouse on the gorge at Craigflower. Still standing, Craigflower School is one of a number of buildings erected by a group of twenty-five families who emigrated from England in 1853. Close by is the great log manor house of Kenneth McKenzie, bailiff for the Puget's Sound Agricultural Company and overseer of Craigflower Farm. This small community soon boasted a sawmill, flour mill, brick kiln, a number of service shops, a general store and a bakery for supplying biscuits to the Navy. Lumber for the schoolhouse was whipsawn on the site, and bricks were made locally—all except those imported from England to construct the 6-foot-wide fireplaces. Locks and hinges too were English-made, and the bell from a wrecked steamboat, suspended in a free-standing timber framework, summoned the children to school and the parishioners to chapel.

In 1856, Christ Church, known as the Victoria District Church, was constructed by Governor Douglas to serve H.B.C. personnel and the local settlers. Its first incumbent was the company's chaplain, Rev. Edward Cridge, who preached there until the church burned down in 1869. This year also marked the first influx of miners from California and the east, enticed by reports of gold discoveries on the Fraser River. As Douglas moved quickly to declare British sovereign rights on the mainland, Cridge appealed to the

Colonial and Continental Church Society in England for more clergy to assist him. Colonization of Vancouver Island had sparked an interest in the Pacific Northwest by the three great missionary societies of Great Britain: the Church Missionary Society, the Society for the Propagation of the Gospel, and the Colonial and Continental Church Society. They saw Vancouver Island and the mainland as a promising field for ministering to the settlers and evangelizing the native Indians. William Duncan of the C.M.S. was already at work at Fort Simpson when Cridge's plea brought as reinforcements Rev. W. Burton Crickmer (C.C.C.S.) of Oxford, Rev. Richard Dowson, and James Gammage (S.P.G.). A few months later, in January 1860, the first bishop of the new colony, Rev. George Hills, formerly vicar of Great Yarmouth, arrived in Victoria. He was to serve his parishioners and church for thirty-two years, administering the Anglican see of British Columbia, witnessing B.C.'s entry into Confederation and the expansion of his church into all areas of the province.

Bishop Hills, the son of an English admiral, was an aristocrat, well educated and an eloquent speaker. As a ritualist, he favoured greater formality and ceremony in the church service, and vigorously opposed discrimination against immigrant American coloured people in religious affairs. His good judgement generally prevailed, and after four months at his new post he had established a collegiate school for boys, taken important steps towards ministering to the Indians, and laid the cornerstone for the first and only prefabricated iron church in the colony—St. John's.

Hills's arrival in Victoria was largely due to the generous sponsorship of Miss (later Baroness) Angela Burdett-Coutts. The daughter of Sir Francis Burdett and granddaughter of Thomas Coutts, the famous London banker, she became, at twenty-three, the richest woman in England. At first savouring the delights of the city's social life, she soon gave up her debutante status and turned instead to endowing churches at home and abroad, financing bishoprics as far afield as Adelaide, Capetown and Victoria. Miss Burdett-Coutts launched the diocese of British Columbia with a £15,000 donation and later, having become the chief benefactress of the Anglican Church in the new colony, enjoyed the distinction of having a college (Angela College) and two streets (Burdett Avenue and Coutts Way) named after her in Victoria. She died in 1906 at the age of ninety-two, the first woman to be elevated to the peerage by Queen Victoria.

Before leaving England, Bishop Hills had arranged for the manufacture of a corrugated and cast-iron structure to be delivered, ready for assembly, to the Colony of Vancouver Island. He had persuaded himself that wood would be scarce in the area and accordingly convinced his benefac-

CRAIGFLOWER SCHOOL

tress, Miss Burdett-Coutts, of the need for a prefabricated church and clergy house in his new bishopric. Hills was a man of his age, and a Gothic edifice in iron was the height of Victorian fashion, possessing the important ecclesiastical qualities of the day—practicality and elegance. Joseph Paxton's Crystal Palace, housing Prince Albert's great Trade and Industry Exhibition of 1851, had captured the interest of the Ecclesiological Society, and five years later William Slater, an Ecclesiologist and architect, published designs for an iron church in the document *Instrumenta Ecclesiastica*. He described the structure as follows:

The external walls are a framework of cast iron, so arranged as to have the interstices faced internally and externally with corrugated plates, and packed between with felt and sand. The arches (lateral and transverse), the framework of the roofs, and the girders of the aisles are formed of iron castings riveted together.... The columns, instead of being cast imitations of stone forms, are composed of four detached rods bound together by a spiral band.

St. John's, of similar design, was prefabricated at a factory in Norwich, England, was shipped around the Horn, and arrived in Esquimalt in early 1860. The building was erected soon after at the corner of Douglas and Fisgard streets. Bishop Hills exclaimed of the consecration, "I felt most thankful that in five months from the laying of the [corner]stone this goodly edifice should be reared. It will, I am sure, revive religion amongst us."

From the outset St. John's was acoustically deficient, blessed with a capacity to amplify outside noises. As one observer recounted,

If a storm came up during the service, the wind rattled the iron roof like thunder and the rain sounded like machine gun fire. At the peak of a storm there would be moans and shrieking noises and only the organ could compete with the sound.... The minister didn't have a chance.

Despite this problem, and despite the somewhat dark and sombre interior, the church served its parishioners well and remained in use, on the site now occupied by the Hudson's Bay Company department store, until demolished in 1913. Remnants of its heavy corrugated walls can still be found on a Public Works building behind the Queen's Printer, off Superior Street.

Preceding the Anglican Bishop were the Wesleyan Methodists, led by Dr. Ephraim Evans. Arriving in 1859, he and three others from eastern Canada—the Reverends Edward White, Ebenezer Robson and Arthur Browning—formed the main contingent for the West Coast mission. They were soon to be joined in Victoria by the Presbyterians, the Congregationalists, the Unitarians, the Quakers, an active Jewish congregation, and, in the late 1870s, the Baptists. Browning departed for Nanaimo and established, with incumbent Cornelius Bryant, a district church and Indian school; White was stationed at New Westminster; Robson ministered to the new towns of Hope and Yale, and Evans directed his efforts towards the Indian and Chinese missions and the building of a great wooden church, First Methodist, in Victoria. The congregation commissioned the new colony's most proficient architect, John Wright, to draw up plans for this structure. He provided them with a rusticated Gothic church, typical of those being erected in England, Upper Canada and San Francisco. The *Victoria Gazette* described the design on 23 July 1859:

It is of the Gothic style of architecture... and will be erected on the lot forming a corner of Pandora and Broad Streets. The first floor will contain fifty-six pews, in three circular rows, capable of seating comfortably three hundred persons. The stone basement will be fitted up for a school and lecture room. [A tower] with a height of one hundred and twenty feet from the ground... is in the center of the front.

Wright was a master of many architectural styles. His buildings were Italianate, Richardsonian-Romanesque, or Gothic Revival, as the occasion demanded. In First Methodist he pursued the principles of Welby Pugin, much as Ferry was to do in Christ Church a dozen years later. Reassuring strength and delightful skill emanate from the crafted woodwork of the hammer-beam ceiling, the roof pinnacles and ornamental gables, and the heavenward-pointing spire of that great central tower.

Christ Church was replaced in 1872. Bishop Hills, by now a true Ruskinian, believed that stone, not wood, best befitted a House of God. While in England he commissioned architect Benjamin Ferry, a member of the Ecclesiological Society and a follower of the influential English architect Welby Pugin, to draw up plans for a stone cathedral. The building was to be 24 feet wide by 80 feet long, with north and south side aisles, flanked on both sides of its western façade by "massive and lofty towers." The roof was to be wood timbers and shingles and the main walls and "bold arches" local limestone with freestone dressings. Ferry's high Victorian Gothic design proved too expensive, and a wooden church, designed by Lieutenant Governor Joseph Trutch—a surveyor and engineer—was eventually erected. Asymmetrical in composition, with a dominating tower and supported by false buttresses, its interior displayed light and graceful columns, a flamboyant hammer-beam ceiling structure, and the decorative details and windows envisioned in Ferry's design. Today a third Christ

St. John's Anglican, the Iron Church (PABC)

Interior of the Iron Church (PABC)

First Methodist, Victoria (PABC)

Joseph Trutch's Christ Church Cathedral (1872) (PABC)

QUADRA STREET CEMETERY, VICTORIA, WITH CHRIST CHURCH BEYOND

Church, constructed of stone, begun in 1926 and still unfinished, stands one block east of the original site, adjacent to the old Quadra Street Cemetery. Here the tombstones of H.B.C. chief factors and early pioneers lie scattered among stately Garry oaks, their weathered surfaces complimenting the sandstone edifice beyond.

†

While the Oblates of Esquimalt served the Indian missions on the Pacific Coast, the Bishop of Vancouver, Rev. Modeste Demers, attended the Catholic needs of the white population in Victoria. In 1857 he journeyed to Lachine in Lower Canada and obtained the services of four Sisters

ished by a master craftsman, Brother Michaud. Constructed in the style of the traditional rural church in Quebec, with its bell cast roof, rose window and clocher, it boasted an elaborate arched ceiling. The vaults, shaped in redwood boards shipped up from San Francisco, were held together with round pegs and, according to the *British Colonist*, "constructed of wood so well matched that it is difficult to discern its joints." Michaud also carved the capitals and bosses of the columns and arches and the five circular ceiling wreathes containing symbols of the cross, the harp, the initials of Ave Maria, and, over the altar, "the Glorypiece gilded like a sun...."

In 1886, the cathedral was threatened with demolition, for it stood on the property of St. Joseph's Hospital. The

An early view of the Roman Catholic mission, Victoria, from Christ Church Cathedral. Photo by R. Maynard (PABC)

from the Institute of St. Ann. One year later, having travelled through New York, Panama City and San Francisco, they arrived in Victoria to establish the first Catholic school for the daughters of the white settlers and the employees of the Hudson's Bay Company. The Sisters' initial course of studies included reading, writing, arithmetic, bookkeeping, geography, grammar, rhetoric, history, English, French and "plain and ornamental needlework"—an ambitious program for a pioneer community. The little two-room school of cedar logs (preserved today in the Provincial Museum gardens) opened in November and the pupils included both rich and poor. The daughters of the Governor, Alice, Agnes and Martha Douglas, are reported in attendance, along with numerous "half breed and coloured children." Close to the little school (**A**), on six city lots near Beacon Hill, Demers built his own house (**B**), the first hospital (**C**), and (**D**) a new church—St. Andrew's Cathedral.

Dedicated in 1858, St. Andrew's was designed and fin-

Sisters of St. Ann, however, who by this time had opened new schools in Cowichan, New Westminster, Mission, Williams Lake and Nanaimo, were intent on saving the old building. Their devoted work had yielded great rewards, for in 1861 they were able to occupy a brick structure known as the View Street Convent, and ten years later to construct the first segment of the Humbolt Street Convent (**E**), designed to house the Sisters and 150 pupils. Later known as St. Ann's Academy, it is no longer in use as a school for girls. Behind the additions of 1886 can be found the old cathedral, relocated, attached to the main buildings and protected by new stone walls. Its fine wood interior is still intact. The orchards, gardens and outbuildings lie deteriorating. Only the great trees forming the cloister walk stand as witness to days when music echoed in the halls and "the pupils all appeared dressed in white muslin (triple flounced), white gloves, blue sashes and belts."

In its greatest days, St. Ann's Academy was the centre of activity for the hard-working Sisters, who eventually

THE FORMER ST. ANDREW'S CATHEDRAL, NOW THE CHAPEL OF ST. ANN

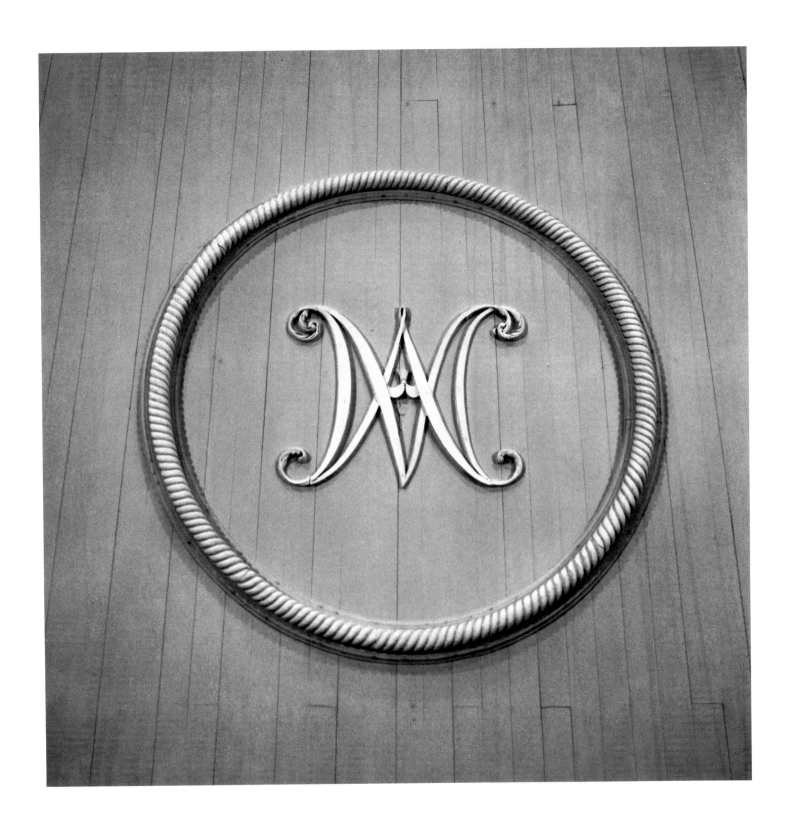

staffed no less than thirty-four schools from British Columbia to Alaska. The cornerstone for the oldest (middle) portion of the convent was laid in 1871 by Lieutenant Governor Joseph Trutch. Designed by architect Charles Vereydhen in the Renaissance revival style, the building displayed classic proportions, Tuscan stone rustication and an exuberant cornice topped with five segmented dormers.

Not much other record remains of Vereydhen. Like many of his colleagues who were unable to attract regular architectural commissions in those competitive days, he advertised in the Victoria *Colonist* as "Carpenter, Contractor and Builder . . . plans and drawings made in every style."

that elegant and commodious edifice to its utmost capacity, and evincing in the most substantial manner the interest and appreciation of the public in the laudable efforts of the congregation. The interior of the building, which is in the Gothic style, and, as the Reverend Mr. Taylor remarked, presents as fine an appearance as anything on the Pacific Coast, is most tastefully decorated, the alcove at the upper end displaying in evergreen the motto "the earth is the Lord's and the fulness thereof," while the lower end showed a beautiful "V.R.", supported on each side by a Prince of Wales' feather. The tables, eight in number, presided over at each end by one of the ladies of the congregation, were beautifully ornamented with flowers, vases, silver plate, etc., and fairly groaned under the weight of

Victoria, looking north up Blanshard Street (PABC)

As Victoria grew in size, other religious denominations began to construct their temples of worship. In 1863, a church precinct was well established at the north end of Blanshard Street, within blocks of the forest's edge. Close to First Methodist and the Iron Church (**A**) were First Presbyterian (**B**) and Emmanu-el, the Jewish Synagogue (**C**). The architect John Wright designed the Presbyterian edifice in Gothic style, constructed of wood, and the synagogue in the Romanesque mode, entirely of brick.

Rev. John Hall of the Irish Church presided at First Presbyterian, which quickly became a highly successful social centre. Both church and churchgoers were described in the *British Colonist*:

Notwithstanding the dark, rainy, muddy state of the weather last night, between four and five hundred people turned out to the soirée in the Presbyterian Church, filling

every possible variety of light and dainty delicacies. . . .

The party broke up about half past ten o'clock, thus terminating perhaps the largest and most successful affair of the kind ever held in Victoria.

Rev. Hall was replaced two years later by Rev. Thomas Sommerville, a Scots Presbyterian. After a property dispute, he started a new church, renamed it St. Andrew's, and took many of the old congregation with him. Both groups flourished over the years until their reunion within the Presbyterian Church of Canada. In 1890, a fine new St. Andrew's of polychrome brick with magnificent stained-glass windows was erected on Douglas Street.

Emmanu-el is still in use, though its brick façade and a splendid three-arched entrance of decorative masonry and marble columns were until recently covered over by a layer of stucco. A classic, two-level gallery interior, vaulted and

ST.ANN'S ACADEMY, VICTORIA

of fine proportions, has been fractured by a mid-level suspended ceiling, but restoration is now (1980) underway, and soon Emmanu-el will rank highly among heritage structures in the historic city.

Angela College, on Burdett Avenue, originally an Anglican girls' school endowed by Baroness Burdett-Coutts, is John Wright's surviving masterwork. It was constructed in 1866 when the architect's practice with George Saunders was well established in San Francisco as well as Victoria. Wright was born in Killearn, Scotland, in 1830 and emigrated as a young man to Guelph, Ontario. Some of his architectural training must have taken place in Upper Canada and he was probably well aware of the work of American architects Frank Wills, Richard Upjohn, John Notman and others who were influenced by the Ecclesiologists. In California, he was admired by his students and known to possess "the largest and most complete architectural library on the coast." Late in his life he was elected first president of the San Francisco Chapter of the American Institute of Architects.

While in Victoria, he designed numerous churches and residences and built the Fisgard Island lighthouse, still operating in Esquimalt harbour. He left for San Francisco one year after the construction of Angela College and there designed several important churches, offices, asylums and college buildings. Of all these, only the stately Romanesque theological seminary at San Anselmo still survives.

Angela College displays all the important characteristics of High Victorian design—asymmetrical composition of forms, polychromatic materials and high-pitched roofs and gables finished with simple geometric stone dressings. In 1908 the building was turned into a hotel and fifty-one years later was sold to the Sisters of St. Ann, who renamed it Mount St. Angela. Today, inhabited by elderly Sisters, it sits peacefully across the street from the imposing mass of Christ Church Cathedral.

In 1872 the issue of ritualism versus evangelical practice within the Anglican Church came to a head. The occasion was the consecration of the second Christ Church Cathedral, and it resulted in the expulsion of Dean Edward Cridge from the English Church, the formation of a new alliance with the Reformed Episcopal Church of America, and, three years later, the construction of the Church of Our Lord. The conflict between Cridge and Bishop Hills became the scandal of the day. The Venerable William Sheldon Reece, Archdeacon of Vancouver, Washington Territory, was invited to preach the evening sermon on the day of consecration, and, with Hills's implicit approval, dealt with the beneficial aspects of the Catholic Revival and the belief that the Church, as an institution, was an instrument of the Divine Will.

He intimated that religious devotion was increased and enhanced by the amount of formal ceremony and ritual in the church service. The fiery Dean, who was in attendance, leapt to his feet and addressed the congregation:

My dearly beloved friends, it is with the greatest shame and humiliation that, as a matter of conscience, I feel it is my duty to say a few words to you before we part. As your pastor, after what we have just heard, I feel it is my duty to raise my voice in protest against it. During the seventeen years that I have officiated as your pastor in this spot, this is the first time ritualism has been preached here, and I pray God Almighty it may be the last. So far as I can prevent it, it shall be the last.

It would appear that the Dean had the majority of the

The Church of Our Lord, Victoria, with pub at left (PABC)

audience on his side, for they approved of his outburst by "clapping of hands and stamping of feet." Cridge had chosen an inopportune moment, however, to protest the sermon's subject matter. With his superiors in attendance, he had shown considerable arrogance, disrespect for his bishop, and was, in fact, guilty of a dangerous breach of canon law. Hills was forced to take action and wrote many letters requesting an apology. Cridge finally replied through the editorial pages of the local press, passionately insisting that the ritualist innovations would leave the church "the hold of every foul spirit and the cage of every unclean bird." In April of 1874 Bishop Hills summoned Cridge before an ecclesiastical court, which promptly found him guilty of sixteen charges including "brawling in church." He was suspended from his duties and, after one last unauthorized service at Christ Church, protected by "groups of muscular Christians," he left the Church of England forever, taking three-quarters of his congregation with him.

The Church of Our Lord, built for Cridge two years later

on land donated by the former Governor of British Columbia, Sir James Douglas, was an instant success. Designed by John Teague and constructed of California redwood, it displayed all the necessary characteristics of High Victorian Gothic—pronounced board and batten rustication, decorated gables, splendid colourful trefoil windows and an expressive hammer beam ceiling. Cridge preached here until his death in 1913. His sermons were recalled by an old Anglican friend, Rev. John Good: "His voice was of a sort which rose and fell with a kind of musical cadence which had the most lulling effect upon his hearers and irresistably charmed them to sleep."

†

St. Paul's, Esquimalt, on its original site (PABC)

Within four months of his arrival in Victoria, Bishop Hills had established Church of England services at Cedar Plains in the outlying rural district of Saanich. In those days he befriended the young Lt. Edmond Verney of the Royal Navy ship *Grappler*, and the two rode out often from Victoria through the rolling countryside to observe the parsonage and the new church under construction. Hills frequently provided services for those on board the ships anchored in Esquimalt harbour, and this association gave him convenient transportation by sea to the parishes of Comox, Nanaimo, Cowichan and North and South Saanich.

The Church of St. Luke, in Cedar Plains, opened on 26 October 1862. An old watercolour (hanging in the church which replaced St. Luke's, at Cedar Hill Cross Road) shows that it resembled St. John the Divine at Yale, designed by that architect of all styles, John Wright. After the consecration, Hills wrote in his diary:

I preached from St. James iv:8, "Draw nigh to God." I trust

this little church will be productive of Blessing to the people of this beautiful valley. Many alas, are now careless and of intemperate habits....

Twenty-six years later, Hills consecrated the replacement church, designed by Edward Mallandaine. Now only old grave monuments and, in springtime, a flock of wild crocuses and daffodils mark the site of the original building.

At Esquimalt is yet another of Hills's churches, St. Paul's —one of the largest and most interesting wooden churches on Vancouver Island. It was constructed in 1866 with funds supplied by the British Admiralty. For the laying of the cornerstone, Bishop Hills invited various clergy, Governor Kennedy, Admiral Denman and his naval officers, and the choir from St. John's Iron Church. The architect, Thomas Trounce, was also in attendance. In the harbour, the gunboat *Forward*, H.M.S. *Sutlej* and *Scout*, and the U.S. war steamer *Saginaw* were dressed in bunting with flags flying.

Over the years the church struggled to make ends meet, for the Admiralty stipend of £50 per year was found insufficient, and visiting navy personnel contributed little to pew rentals. Others were required to pay $5 a year, and the minister of the day often held services aboard ship, taking up a collection to help the struggling church. Still, the local residents enjoyed the participation of the elite body of men, if the minister, Rev. W.W. Bolton, who served St. Paul's from 1887 to 1889, is to be believed:

The attendance of Bluejackets... was a delightful sight, the little church crammed to the door, the civilians having no trouble at all to get inside, the singing amazing in its volume, the service going with a swing.

St. Paul's is a Gothic parish church and contains some of the finest glass windows and oak carvings in the province. Small diamond-shaped glass panes in blues and mauves were made in London and shipped around the Horn in 1878. A beautiful three-light window in the sanctuary, which depicts scenes from the life of Christ, was given in memory of Alice, the second daughter of Rev. H.P. Wright, who was rector of St. Paul's from 1876 to 1880. Another window, showing Joshua and Solomon, honours Governor Frederick Seymour, who died on shipboard at Bella Coola under mysterious circumstances in 1869. A unique rose window with an anchor at its centre is located over the baptismal font. Strongly carved oak relief embellishes the pulpit and post capping. This fine work was carried out in 1930 by W.E.A. Barclay, who dedicated it to the memory of his father, Canon W.G. Barclay of Salisbury, England. On the walls are plaques in memory of sailors who have lost their

ST. LUKE'S CHURCH, CEDAR HILL CROSS ROAD

MOUNT ST. ANGELA, THE FORMER ANGELA COLLEGE FOR GIRLS, VICTORIA

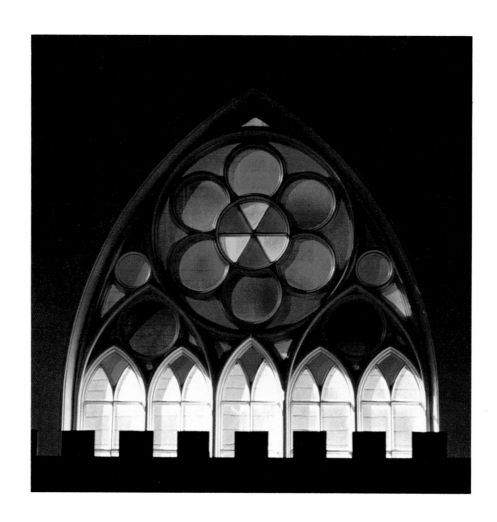

CHURCH OF OUR LORD, VICTORIA

66

ST. PAUL'S, ESQUIMALT

lives at sea, and there is a life ring from H.M.S. *Condor*, which vanished after leaving Esquimalt in a heavy sea on 3 December 1901.

St. Paul's is now relocated up the road from its original site. It sits peacefully in an old orchard, where it was moved in 1903 to avoid the vibrations and damage created by constant gunnery practice on nearby Signal Hill.

Across the Esquimalt harbour, a mile and a half west of the Fisgard lighthouse, lies the Royal Naval Chapel and cemetery. Constructed in 1868, the little sanctuary is still in use and retains much of its original character. Unlike the sturdy lighthouse, built of brick brought around the Horn from England, the Naval chapel was constructed of wood and plaster of a most spartan design. The architect, Edward Mallandaine, originally clad his frame structure in vertical board-and-batten siding and graced the interior with four long benches set against the side walls, perpendicular to a simple square chancel. Today, the exterior has been resurfaced with horizontal clapboard, but the original doors and windows remain intact. Here too are many plaques in memory of British officers, seamen and marines who lost their lives at sea. In the graveyard, countless monuments of stone and teak, some carved aboard ship by fellow seamen, honour those of the ironclad battleship H.M.S. *Zealous*, the paddle-sloop *Hecate* and other great ships which protected British interests on the Northwest Coast.

At Metchosin, twelve miles from the heart of Victoria, is perhaps the most English of this English island's Anglican parish churches, known as St. Mary the Virgin. In springtime the churchyard is filled with dogtooth violets, the delicate blooms erupting among the stately Garry oaks which surround the simple black and white church. Until its construction in 1873, the pioneer settlers of the area held services in private homes and in the schoolhouse. It is another of Edward Mallandaine's churches, and the architect was present at the laying of the foundation stone. He was in select company, for attending the ceremony were the Bishop of Columbia George Hills, Lieutenant Governor Joseph Trutch, and Sir James Douglas, who had headed the building fund committee.

In this period of his life, Mallandaine was enjoying a healthy practice, having spent the previous fifteen years in a variety of enterprises, including what he had advertised as "legal and ornamental writing," teaching drawing, bill collecting, and publishing Victoria city directories. His father too had led an unsettled life. Major Mallandaine, one-time Governor of Singapore and holder of a seat in Fairhill, England, lost his fortune through a venture in the soap business and was forced to move to France, "the object being cheap living and education" for his son. Soon

after, young Mallandaine articled with a London firm, learning the "art and mystery" of architecture by copying most of the plans and documents in the office. He left England with an extensive portfolio of work, took up drafting in Australia, returned to Great Britain to marry, then set out via New York and Panama for the gold rush town of Sacramento. Here, in his words, he "replenished his money," and in 1858 he arrived in Victoria. Five years later he opened an architectural office on Yates Street and advertised as a maker of "designs and working drawings."

His plans for St. Mary the Virgin were approved by Bishop Hills and a tender was let for construction to Messrs. Simpson & Tippins for $1,321. The settlers of Metchosin supplied the hewn foundation timbers and hauled building materials, which were brought by boat from Victoria to the beach at nearby Albert Head. The pews, lectern, pulpit and baptismal font were carved of cedar and are still in use. Scissor trusses support the roof of the 22' x 53' church and the walls are finished in plaster with a fir strip wainscot. A delicately inscribed Gothic arch frames the chancel and the diamond panes of the sanctuary window.

John Witty of Metchosin, who contributed the land for the church, met with a fatal accident on the day of the building's consecration, but it was otherwise a joyous occasion. Douglas recorded the scene in a letter to his daughter:

Metchosin looked its best, the beautiful slopes, the richly tinted foliage, the bright clear sky, the warm sunshine, the glassy, smooth sea and the grand mountains in the distance, formed a combination of indescribable beauty. I felt an exhilaration of mind which led me to wander away through the woods towards the white cliffs bordering the sea from whence I contemplated its placid waters with delight.

The site and the building are as splendid today, and St. Mary the Virgin continues as the centre of activity in the quiet community.

One of the oldest and most picturesque Anglican churches on the Saanich Peninsula stands on Mount Newton Cross Road near Saanichton. Surrounded by tranquil fields and farmhouses, St. Stephen's was built on seven acres of land, presented in part by William Thompson, the first white settler in the area. Thompson moved to the district in 1855 after surviving a stormy entry into the new colony. Enroute from San Francisco to Victoria, his ship foundered off the west coast of Vancouver Island near Pachena Point. Thompson fell into the hands of the Nitinat Indians and eventually stumbled into the village of

ST. PAUL'S, ESQUIMALT

ROYAL NAVAL CHAPEL, ESQUIMALT
Opposite: ST. MARY THE VIRGIN, METCHOSIN

THE CHURCH OF THE ASSUMPTION, WEST SAANICH
Opposite: ST. STEPHEN'S, WEST SAANICH

Esquimalt clothed only in a loincloth of bark. He was grateful to be alive.

A ship's carpenter by trade, Thompson fell in love with the Saanich countryside and turned to farming. In 1862, he built St. Stephen's of redwood imported from California. Its style, again similar to that of St. John the Divine at Yale, was designed by Wright & Sanders of Victoria and built the same year. Bishop Hills attended the opening of the church, and preached to villagers and some sixty persons who rode out on horseback and in carriages from Victoria. He noted that there was hearty singing, many true prayers and a good collection. On Christmas Day the same year, Thompson planted two fir trees on either side of the entrance porch "to give the new little edifice a holiday aspect." Today, they tower high above the roof, their roots supporting the building's foundation.

In 1877 St. Stephen's was renovated and enlarged, and a cemetery was consecrated. Distinctive side buttresses were later added, giving it a solid, substantial look. All the interior fittings are made of oak and mahogany, and a Gothic stained-glass window lights the chancel. Long misty green strands of lichen cling to the ancient trees in the graveyard, and many of the crumbling tombstones are encrusted with moss and fungi. Bright buttercups and cow parsley abound in summer, and the once-small ornamental cypress trees have grown up lopsided over many of the graves and their crusty iron fences. In this season the handsome lich-gate, one of the few in the province which survive, is covered in clematis and wild honeysuckle.

Across the rolling fields from St. Stephen's stands the Roman Catholic Church of the Assumption. Constructed in 1869, it was probably the third place of worship to be erected by the Romanists to serve the South Saanich Indians and the new farming community. Nine years earlier, Brother Blanchet and Father Joyal, who had recently left the Nisqually Mission on Puget Sound, erected a rough shelter on the reserve overlooking the Saanich Inlet. The next year, a permanent chapel and priest's house was built of logs. The Church of the Assumption is of simple, classic proportions, with a carpenter Gothic tower located at the rear of the building—apparently directed towards those approaching the sanctuary by water. Ironically it is the Anglican Bishop Hills who has left us the most detailed description of the work of the priests in the village.

Mats were laid over the floor, a bell was rung through the village and the people came in. . . . The chief's son, a youth of fifteen, read the service in a monotone. It seemed to be the Roman Catholic vesper service. He recited the priest's part, and the people in loud unison took theirs. There was the creed, Ave Maria, confession, and a hymn. They beat their breasts at the confession, and crossed themselves at another part. The bell rang several times. The ceremony lasted about twenty minutes, and much of the service was in their own language. We could not help feeling that if in so short a time these Indians could be schooled to this exercise, there was promise of their docility in receiving our purer faith.

The Catholic missionaries were the first Christians active in the fertile Cowichan Valley and for many years faithfully ministered to the Indian tribes in the district. The English Church, in contrast, attended to the "European resident population," and the first Anglican incumbent, Rev. W.S. Reece, was quick to point out the difficulties of dealing with the natives, noting problems of

St. Peter's Church, Quamichan (PABC)

migratory habits, language barriers, loose morals and the ever-present Catholic Church.

Reece served the settlers in the large agricultural districts of Shawnigan, Koksilah, Somenos, Quamichan, Cowichan, Comiaken, Chemainus, and Salt Spring Island, By March 1866, in all this area, the Church of England could claim only a mission school-chapel on the edge of Somenos Lake. Reece held services there, in his parsonage, and at the John Bull Inn on Cowichan Bay. He was forced to ford rivers, skirt lakes and travel great distances to reach his parishioners. By October Bishop Hills had granted funds for the construction of a log church at Quamichan, and on Lent Sunday, in February 1867, the first service was held. The congregation numbered forty-two, and they attended a church of the "simplest and plainest character." Reece noted that the furnishings consisted of an altar, a lectern, a reading desk, open benches and a stove.

Ten years later a frame church, St. Peter's, was raised on the same site by Rev. David Holmes, who had succeeded

ST. PETER'S, QUAMICHAN

Reece after the latter preached a controversial sermon at Victoria. Holmes commissioned Edward Mallandaine to design his church, a portion of which remains today. Additions have lengthened the structure, and handsome trusses within now terminate in a pinwheel formation in the ceiling of the western apse. Stained-glass windows enrich the nave and sanctuary, and a beautifully carved lid, in the form of a spire, graces the baptismal font. The graveyard, which rambles down the grassy slope away from the church, contains the remains of many pioneers, including those of the grandson of William and Frances Barkley (of

St. Paul's Episcopal, Nanaimo (PABC)

the famous British fur trading vessel *Imperial Eagle*), three provincial premiers of the 1880s and '90s, and William Duncan, for whom the nearby town of Duncan was named. Magnificent oaks and conifers link the cemetery and the wooden church into elegant harmony.

Across the Sansum Narrows on Salt Spring Island, other Anglican settlers built churches in later years. St. Mark's at Ganges was the first, built in 1889 by Samuel Beddis and his son Charles, and dedicated three years later by Bishop Hills. St. Mary's, at Fulford Harbour, was constructed soon after to serve the settlers of the Burgoyne Valley. Rev. J. Belton Haslam, the first resident clergyman on Salt Spring Island, drew up the plans, and in 1894 his successor, Rev. E.F. Wilson, called a community "bee" and started construction. According to the parish magazine the total cost

of the frame structure was $750, including the seating, chancel fittings and organ. For fifteen years Rev. Wilson kept a firm grip on his parishioners, travelling to their homes by horse and buggy and dispensing a strict "old-time" religion. An impressive sight in his black cloth and long dark beard, he read from his great Bible and, if called upon, provided medical advice and assistance when a doctor was not available. His vicarage was built at the back of the church and here he maintained a well-kept garden. Today, the church and its outbuildings are surrounded by wild grasses and ornamental trees, with an old lich gate and headstones marking the resting place of many Salt Spring pioneers.

†

In 1852 James Douglas, later Governor Douglas, later Sir James, was Chief Factor of the Hudson's Bay Company in Victoria. In this capacity he sent his representative Joseph Mackay on an important mission to Nanaimo:

You will proceed with all possible diligence to Wentuhuysen Inlet, commonly known as Nanymo Bay, and formally take possession of the coal beds lately discovered there....

The new colony and the great steamships of the day required plenty of "the black rock" for fuel, and where the company went the church would surely follow. Within two years a new community was burgeoning, and fifty tons of coal a day were being taken from a bed near the site of the present Malaspina Hotel.

The Methodists, led by Cornelius Bryant, a lay reader, were the first religious group on the scene. Bryant ministered to and taught the Nanaimo Indians, who soon built a small frame church on the reserve. In 1860 he and Rev. Arthur Browning erected First Methodist of wood, in the Tuscan style. Within a year, the Anglicans, under Rev. J.B. Good, had constructed a "rustic chapel for native worship" and the Church of St. Paul's on Dallas Square, in the centre of town. This wooden church of fine proportions was, Good said, his "first love," from which he moved on to serve sixteen years with the Indians on the Thompson River. "It was an English architect who supplied the plans, for which we paid twenty-five pounds and which might well serve as a model of what a church ought to be...."

As new coal seams were discovered and worked, and as the town grew to a population of 500, the Hudson's Bay Company sold its interests to the Vancouver Coal Mining and Land Company. The sum of £100,000 bought "6,193 acres of land and the underlying coal, together with 100 dwellings, houses, stores, workshops, machinery, powerful steam engines, wharfs, barges and a sawmill."

ST. MARY'S, FULFORD HARBOUR

ST. ANNE'S, ALDERMERE

A new town plan was drawn up in England and streets were laid out radiating from the peninsula on which the early buildings stood. Lots were sold by auction in Victoria, and in 1864 the Gothic-revival Roman Catholic Church of St. Peter's was erected. Two years later, Rev. Robert Jamieson of the Church of Scotland constructed First Presbyterian on property across the ravine from the old centre—the first of numerous places of worship to be built in that part of the rapidly expanding town.

St. Anne's, Aldermere, located near French Creek, twenty-four miles north of Nanaimo, was raised in 1894. Although late in coming, it was the first church of the little farming district of Englishman River, later known as Parksville. In 1892, the community consisted of twenty families and boasted a store-hotel, a red schoolhouse, and a log post office—the latter still preserved and relocated on the Columbia Beach Estate. The Reverend Charles Cooper served the area and the adjacent settlements at Nanoose, Qualicum Beach and Coombs. In 1890, determined to build a new church, he bought a site and donated it to the community through the Anglican Synod at Victoria. The parishioners rose to the challenge, and four years later they had cleared the site and felled the great cedar trees destined to form the walls. The interior, contrasting sharply with the rugged hand-adzed exterior, is lined with dark, oiled clapboard siding. This sombre space is highlighted by one rich burst of colour, the sanctuary window, sent from England by Mr. E.B. May, a former parishioner.

Today St. Anne's is well maintained by an active congregation. It stands proudly on its original site among the tombstones of the pioneers who built it and who worshipped there in years gone by.

Some forty miles farther north, the Comox Valley has for many years been blessed with ideal land for cultivation. By 1862 the area had over four thousand arable acres free from timber, and of these the Church of England held 170 in the most central location. Here, on the banks of the Puntledge River, a log chapel and mission house were erected in 1864 by the attendant catechist, J.C.B. Cave, and his parishioners. Cave, who was proud of his cooking, recorded the action:

There were five men on the building and three on the ground and two inside. The building went up well, and without a single murmur from one present. I was busily engaged all morning, cooking and arranging house, collecting together plates, etc. for them, and at twelve o'clock they all sat down to a fried salmon with onion sauce and two large vegetable dishes full of potatoes. They all went to work again after dinner and finished all the building, with the exception of the two top logs, right round.

Seven years later, the Reverend Jules Xavier Willemar and his lay assistant, Mr. H. Guillod, left their West Coast post at Port Alberni and arrived in Comox to establish a more permanent mission. They found the old log building in bad repair. The mud chimney had collapsed, the walls and broken windows offered little protection from wind and rain, and ferns grew thick and tall through the floor boards. In 1873 Willemar built a school-chapel on the Indian reserve and three years later erected St. Andrew's, Sandwick, on higher ground at the foot of Mission Hill. Acreage was donated on the hill above for a cemetery, and Bishop Hills travelled by ship to the little community to open both building and burial ground. Some of the windows of the old log chapel were reused in St. Andrew's. Skilled woodworkers carved the furnishings and the pews. The original handmade lamps in metal sconces still provide light in the building.

Rev. Willemar, concerned that the church had no bell, remembered the sinking of the Australian ship *Lady Blackwood* on the rocks near Port Alberni. He resolutely set out on foot over the rugged mountains of the Beaufort Range and salvaged the ship's bell, which rings today from the steeple of St. Andrew's. He led his congregation for forty-two years and died at the age of ninety-one, leaving a spiritual legacy well remembered today.

†

In 1858 came the first rush of miners to the lower Fraser, and James Douglas, newly appointed Governor of the Colony of British Columbia, moved to establish an effective presence on the mainland for the British crown. He chose Derby, the former site of old Fort Langley, as the colonial capital. Within the year, lots were advertised for sale for $100 and the Reverend William Burton Crickmer of Oxford was called from England to take charge of a new ministry. Soon after his arrival at Derby in February 1859 he wrote to the Colonial and Continental Church Society:

Your missionary preached the very first regular sermon in the colony of British Columbia.... My church was a half-furnished barrack, my congregation soldiers and civilians, my pulpit a Union Jack over a box, and my text Genesis 1:27, "The New Creation."

Crickmer had been appointed chaplain to the Royal Engineers under Col. Richard Clement Moody, who had been sent out to establish law and order and assist in the development of the new colonies. At Derby, Crickmer constructed a parsonage and a church of redwood, following the design of his old parish church in London, St. John the Divine. Bishop Hills, in May 1860, described a visit to the

ST. ANDREW'S, SANDWICK: THE CEMETERY & THE CHURCH BEYOND

little church, finished inside with bird's-eye maple and redwood.

Derby. Here the church is in good order... length about 52... breadth about 22...; 28 [persons] at 5 sittings each = 140. The Parsonage is small — 3 rooms and a kitchen.

Our two Indians paddled us down the stream in good time. The motion is very delightful. The day was fine, the scenery enlivening. We reached the Camp [Derby] a little before 3 — having come 17 miles in rather less than 3 hours. Our Indian in command would sometimes stop paddling and point to spots where he and his tribe once roamed in possession. Now a hostile tribe occupied the land of his fathers. He did not speak of the intrusion of the white man. The fact is, these tribes have suffered far more from each other than they ever can from the Whites.

St. John's, Derby (1859), drawn by Rev. Crickmer (ACV)

Crickmer was a prolific artist and he left behind sketches of his home life, the Church of St. John, and drawings depicting his preaching atop a beer barrel at a gold miners' camp on a Fraser River sand spit. His stay, however, was short-lived. Only two months after the town's inauguration, Colonel Moody condemned the site on sanitary, commercial, military and political grounds, and named Queensborough, or New Westminister, the new capital. Crickmer and his family were transferred to Yale, and his church lay deserted until 1882, when the Anglican congregation at Maple Ridge cut the structure into segments, floated it across the river and hoisted it to a new site with rollers, bull teams and windlasses. The building is today partially restored, though it has been shortened by almost half. Insofar as it survives at all, it is the eldest surviving church on the British Columbia mainland.

As the Maple Ridge District flourished and grew, other churches were built, the most permanent being St. Andrew's Presbyterian, constructed at Haney in 1888 and clad in brick. It was Thomas Haney, farmer, brickmaker and Roman Catholic, who, after helping build his own church, donated the land on Calligan Street for St. Andrew's. Haney learned his trade in Ontario and came to Maple Ridge in 1876 looking for clay suitable for brick manufacturing. He found it on the Wickwire Estate, promptly purchased 160 acres for $1000, and there constructed a brickyard which he operated for eleven years. His home still stands one block east of St. Andrew's on Ontario Street. The old church — covered with brick donated from the numerous brickyards which developed in the area — now sits empty, its steep wooden roof covered in moss, its windows boarded over and its lower walls deteriorating. Proposed restorations will bring new usefulness to this historic structure.

Across the river at Derby, a stone cairn marks the old townsite which witnessed the beginnings of permanent settlement on the mainland. At its edge the Fraser surges, lead-grey and relentless, towards the sea.

Col. Richard Clement Moody's great importance in the history of British Columbian architecture stems from his position as Officer in Charge of the Columbia Detachment of the Royal Engineers. He and his 165 officers and men — the Sappers — had been dispatched to the West Coast by the British Colonial Secretary, Sir Edward George Bulwer-Lytton, to provide evidence of royal power and to open up the resources of the unorganized territory. Like Douglas, Lytton was alarmed at the influx of miners, "this motley inundation of immigrant diggers," as he called them, and he was determined that the gold seekers would not take over New Caledonia as he felt the land seekers had taken over Oregon. The Engineers were a select group, chosen for intelligence, loyalty, and for skills in various trades and crafts. Thoughtful about their role in developing the new country, they wrote and published their own newspaper while rounding the Horn in 1858 in the clipper ship *Thames City.* "British Columbia," they wrote,

like Australia and California before it, will soon be crowded with a vast and motley throng from nearly every portion of the inhabited globe, attracted thither in search of gold. The first thing to be done is to establish a capital town, accessible if possible to shipping, which, like all other capital towns, shall form the seat of government, a place of habitation and trade, and a depot for the vast stock of stores and provisions necessary to meet the demands of so large a population. The choice of a site on which to establish this capital rests with Colonel Moody, R.E., and there is little doubt that he has ere this decided on the spot, one probably on the banks of the river Fraser. Our first business on our arrival there will be to build houses for

THE CHURCH OF ST. ANDREW AT HANEY

ourselves; then probably, as is the case in all places where Englishmen collect, will appear two or three grog shops, then a store or two, a Government House, a bank, a church, a burial ground, an hotel, a jetty, and finally a street. In due time, too, we shall probably have our theatre, our library, water works, gas works, docks, pavements, lamp-posts, omnibusses, and possibly even railroad and electric telegraphs, the same as in any other civilized town in England. The duties of the detachment will probably be as various as the names of the men composing it, such as clearing and levelling ground, building, draining, roadmaking, surveying, digging wells, building jetties, etc. We shall also have our architects, clerks, surveyors, draughtsmen,

a veranda—the fashionable architectural appointments of the day.

Surveys and master planning for the Royal City got underway with a view to publishing the plans and publicly selling the lands. Both Lytton and Douglas looked to land revenues as the means to finance the Engineers' work in the two colonies. The towns of Lytton, Hope and Yale, and later Douglas, Lillooet, Clinton, Quesnel Forks, Richfield, Barkerville and others were surveyed and blocked out for land sale. Trails and roads to the new towns and gold fields were assessed and upgraded, and the first government buildings, usually the courthouse and local jail, were constructed in each centre. A typical

New Westminster, circa 1863 (PABC)

photographers, and be, we hope, at the bottom of all the good and as little of the evil as possible that is done in the colony.

After building barracks at Derby, the Engineers set to work constructing a permanent camp at Sapperton, just upriver from New Westminster, close to where the old B.C. Penitentiary stands today. At the water's edge, they located Colonel Moody's residence (**A**), the officers' quarters, a storehouse and boat house. On the slope behind, they constructed barracks, a hospital, a club room and library, the Lands and Works offices, a small school and a log church (**B**) which was described by the *Victoria Gazette* as of "a most singular and clumsy appearance." Of better design was Moody's residence, planned by the company's chief architect, Lt. Arthur Lempriere, and his draftsman, Cpl. John Clayton White. The building consisted of a classic "I" plan with a steep Gothic roof, bay windows and

approach to planning was to determine the location of any existing buildings, roads and large natural features and to accommodate them wherever possible. Government reserves for military defence and expansion were located around the town periphery and a gridiron of streets and blocks laid down over the entire site. Most towns were provided with one wide street, "wide enough to turn around a six-yoke mule team without backing." Often a main square was located and surrounded by a number of church reserves, with the Church of England usually granted the first and most prominent site.

In laying out the capital city, New Westminster, the Engineers expressed the stately planning principles of the day. A linear development, parallel to the Fraser River, was terminated at the west end by Dock Square and at the east by Albert Crescent, patterned after the crescents at Bath and Brighton. The wide main street, close to the busy activities at the river's edge, was punctuated by a series of merchant, market and ceremonial squares. Eight church reserves were located throughout the lower town, accommodating all denominations. With its English street names, numerous parks and terraced housing sites, vistas to "Surrey" and horse trails to "New Brighton," the city epitomized Moody's desire to impose an English morality on the untamed land.

The capital's main focus was to be the extensive, centrally located government and public gardens. Moody decided to place the Anglican Cathedral "as an ornamental feature" in the centre of Victoria Gardens, fully realizing the importance of the site, both to the city's appearance from the river approach and to its social life. Lempriere—

Holy Trinity, New Westminster. Photo by R. Maynard (PABC)

now a captain—and Corporal White prepared the plans, and on 8 December 1860, Holy Trinity was consecrated by the ubiquitous Bishop Hills. The church was full and the congregation included the incumbent Rev. John Sheepshanks, five visiting clergy, and members of the Royal Engineers, who provided the choir. The *New Westminster Times* described the new structure.

The edifice, which commands a lovely view of the river, mountains, and surrounding scenery, is built in the early style of Gothic Architecture. . . .

The interior consists of a nave, two aisles, chancel, vestry, and recess for organ. The uprights and rafters are of fir, massive pillars with Gothic arches between, a series of arches also spanning the nave and giving a rich and ecclesiastical appearance to the whole. The internal fittings are of the handsomest description. The seats, which have been presented by various individuals whose hearts warmed

towards the completion of the good work, are of fir, trimmed with the famous California redwood. The lectern or bible-desk (a gift) is of fir and the Columbian cottonwood; the poppy heads of redwood are admirably contrasted, and present an exceedingly rich and elegant appearance. The communion rails, designed by one of the Royal Engineers, are beautifully executed. The whole building reflects the highest credit both upon the taste of the committee, who approved of the plans (presented by Captain A.R. Lempriere, R.E.,) and upon the builders, Messrs. Manson and White, who have performed their part in a truly workmanlike and skillful manner.

Rev. Sheepshanks attended to his duties in those early years with dedication and a sense of humour. His parsonage was a log hut built by two miners close to the church and measured 7' x 10'. Whiskey bottles, with which the builders had filled notches cut in the logs for windows, were soon removed and a curtain of calico on a sliding frame was all that served to keep out the cold of night. Sheepshanks noted that the dwelling was planned to keep housework to a minimum. "I can sit on my wooden bunk," he wrote, "and open the window, shut the door, poke the fire in the stove, and get anything down from the shelf without moving."

When in 1863 the Royal Engineers were recalled, only Colonel Moody, his officers, and fifteen Sappers and their families left for England. Over 130 men stayed behind, many taking advantage of the free 150-acre land grant offered to them. Some took to mining, and others moved to Victoria as tradesmen. Most stayed to farm and work in the lower mainland—among them John Clayton White, who became an architectural draftsman with the colonial Department of Lands and Works.

In 1865 Holy Trinity, resplendent with a new 100-foot wooden tower supporting eight cast bronze bells donated by Baroness Burdett-Coutts, burned to the ground. The charred and blackened ruins were rebuilt to designs prepared by architect Hermann Tiedemann of Victoria. Tiedemann, who had planned the picturesque Legislative Buildings in Victoria known as the "Birdcages," decided to build Holy Trinity of stone, quarried from Salt Spring Island. In the great fire of 1898, it too was destroyed, and the present cathedral erected in its place. The old stone walls facing the river were rebuilt as part of the new concrete structure. Today, the elaborate Victoria Gardens envisioned by Moody lie undeveloped and greatly diminished in size. Columbia Street, some major parks and Albert Crescent can be perceived, but the Engineers' grand conception remains sadly unrealized. (Future planners of the city would do well to recognize the old plan's potential.)

As the site of the Royal City was being cleared of its great fir and cedar trees, other denominations began to build in the area. First Wesleyan Methodist, a 30-foot frame building, was built by Rev. Edward White in 1860. A stump too large to remove formed the foundation of one corner of the structure. In 1873, a new church and parsonage were built on the same site.

Also in 1860, Father Léon Fouquet, O.M.I., arrived in New Westminster and immediately set to work clearing the land and building two churches: St. Peter's for the white colonists and St. Charles for the Indians. Young Father Florimond Gendre, who was posted to St. Charles, was to write of those early days:

Close to, if not actually within, the straggling village of the rising capital of British Columbia is the residence of Father Fouquet — if Father Fouquet can be said to have a residence. A roof and bare wooden walls form the shelter for our heads from the rain. In front stands a half-finished church. Two or three hundred yards above, close to the forest, is a still more miserable structure, the Indian chapel.

Father Gendre found himself alone, his only companions the rats which came up from the river below.

When I was cooking, kneading my dough, or baking it on the sheet-iron of my little stove, the entire "community" assisted at the operations. The point of the Rule which I observed the best, after brotherly love, was the prescription of silence. Always strict silence, except when, annoyed by the racket made by the rats, I launched after them some French anathema which the native rodents did not understand.

Later, the Oblates and the Sisters of St. Ann were to build a hospital, a convent and a school for boys in the historic city.

Still standing near the corner of Carnarvon and Merivale streets in New Westminster is the first Presbyterian church built on the mainland. St. Andrew's was constructed in 1863 by the Reverend Robert Jamieson, before his removal to Nanaimo. Its interior has been drastically renovated, but its rusticated, arcaded, board and batten exterior and elegant Regency-Gothic windows remain as originally constructed. These windows are delicately built of thin cedar glazing bars and sheet glass, and no finer examples of the craft exist in the province today. Threatened by age and advancing housing development, this building and its appointments should be saved and a new use found which will ensure its preservation.

Years later, in 1872, Jamieson relocated the old Sapperton schoolhouse to a site two hundred yards south of the old fort at Derby. There it served as a chapel until the congregation built St. Andrew's on Glover Road in 1885. Surrounded by an orchard, this little Victorian church is still used. It stands proudly a few feet away from the town's pioneer cemetery.

At Sapperton itself, in 1865, was constructed a lovely little parish church, St. Mary the Virgin, designed by the former Sapper, John White. Though much altered today, it remains one of the finest examples of wooden Gothic architecture in the province. Eight- by eight-inch vertical timbers and cross bracing define its structural skeleton, and the infill walls are of horizontal clapboard. A steep pitched roof was once topped with a shingled bell cot reminiscent of earlier stone bell turrets constructed in England. Inside, arcaded cedar-panelled walls and age-darkened fir scissor trusses and diagonal planking set the mood for the pageantry and ritual of service. Flags of the empire, the church and the Royal Engineers, and a modern altar cloth, punctuate the chancel and sanctuary space. Here one can sit in the Governor's old pew and contemplate the past — the marriages in this church of many Sappers and their brides, and the baptism here of their children, including those of the architect and his wife Mary, and those of the builder, Daniel Richards, and his wife Mary Ann.

In 1879 the newly appointed Bishop of New Westminster, Acton Windeyer Sillitoe, sat thoughtfully in the same church and wrote in his diary, "St. Mary's Church stands in the grounds of the Archdeaconry House and is a model of what all wooden churches might be and ought to be."

Within three years of St. Mary's construction, the colonies of British Columbia and Vancouver Island were united and Victoria declared the capital. A mass exodus of officials and their families from New Westminister resulted. With great disappointment, the Reverend J.C.B. Cave (whom we met earlier at Comox) wrote in his ledger on 7 June 1868, "The [ship] *Douglas* took away, after morning service, the most of my congregation for their new home," but a few years later, the parish was flourishing once again. It saw its greatest days in the 1880s under Bishop and Mrs. Sillitoe. They were accomplished musicians, and the church soon became a social as well as a religious centre. St. Mary the Virgin still plays as active a role today, having served the busy community for over 112 years.

Opposite: THE CHURCH OF ST. ANDREW AT LANGLEY

THE CHURCH OF ST. MARY THE VIRGIN, SAPPERTON

Gold Trail Missions

Preceding pages: THE CHURCH OF ST. ANDREW, CAYOOSH CREEK;
THE CHURCH OF ST. SAVIOUR, BARKERVILLE, 1868 (PABC)

IN 1856 THE DISCOVERY OF GOLD ONE QUARTER OF A MILE below the confluence of the Thompson and Nicomen rivers sparked British Columbia's great gold rush, and within two years there was feverish mining from the mouth of the Fraser to the high bars above the forks at Lytton. The old Indian trail along the Fraser Canyon wall was virtually impassable beyond Fort Yale, and a shorter and more accessible route was found along the spectacular chain of lakes linking the Fraser River, at the mouth of the Harrison, to Lillooet, 169 miles north. Early travellers walked the distance, aided by the stern-wheeler *Umatilla* on Harrison Lake and later by the *Marzella*, *Lady of the Lake* and *Champion* on Lillooet, Anderson and Seton lakes. The journey was an exasperating one, fraught with delays, difficult terrain and relentless mosquitoes. Improved by the Royal Engineers in 1860 to allow the passage of Fraser River steamers up the Harrison, and also by the introduction of both mules and camels as beasts of burden, the Harrison-Lillooet route was cheerfully abandoned in 1864 in favour of the more recently completed Fraser Canyon/Cariboo Road. Commissioned by Governor Douglas, this great work of engineering and construction opened up the interior of the mainland colony and served both the miners and settlers of the Cariboo until replaced in part in 1884 by yet another monumental work, the C.P.R. Railway.

The development of the Harrison-Lillooet Trail and the Cariboo Road dramatically altered the lives of the Indian people living along these traffic ways. Many served as guides and packers of supplies to the miners and in later years turned to mining, farming, cattle raising and logging. Many of their villages were consolidated into flourishing towns, and today one can observe in their Roman Catholic churches and burial places the last remnants of a unique and indigenous folk art. Other denominations, ministering along these same well-travelled routes, provided sanctuary for a white mining community often unstable and quite irreligious. These churches had limited use, for the miners kept moving on to new gold discoveries or abandoning worked-out claims, but theirs was an original and lasting architecture of utmost simplicity, embellished only through small details such as roof-combs, window and door trim, lattices and railings. A journey to these beautiful and forgotten places serves as a reminder of how important they were to the religious life of the time and how inventive, skillful and determined were their builders.

At a wide bend in the Harrison River, close to where it meets the rushing Fraser, stands the gaunt and partially exposed frame of St. Mary's Church. Situated in the nearly deserted Scowlitz reserve, St. Mary's is at least the second church on this site. Its predecessor withstood the great flood of 1894 at a time when the Scowlitz band were farming, dairying and fishing, and when most of their children attended the Indian school at St. Mary's Mission.

Three miles from this dramatic site, in March of 1860, Capt. John Grant and eighty Royal Engineers deepened the shallow Harrison channel "to admit the passage of steamers of the class at present running the Fraser." By 1862, at the height of the gold rush, perhaps ten thousand miners were working the upper bars of the Fraser, and another five thousand were in the Cariboo. Most had passed this spot, and within twenty to thirty days had reached their destinations—the Quesnel River, or the Eldorado at Lightning, Lowhee and Williams creeks, near fabulous Barkerville.

Port Douglas, with St. Mark's Church at left (PABC)

Fifty miles upstream, at the north end of Harrison Lake and the head of the Harrison-Lillooet Trail, is the site of Port Douglas. Walter Cheadle visited the town in 1862, on his journey across Canada, and described it as "a vile hole in a hollow." Lt. Henry Spencer Palmer of the Royal Engineers, three years earlier, had been equally unenthusiastic about the instant town. "I deem it a very badly chosen spot," he wrote, "and a poor terminus to what is likely to form the main road of communication with the Upper Fraser."

In spite of these comments—which acknowledged the steep terrain and shallow foreshore waters of the site—Colonel Moody and his Engineers proceeded to draw up a town plan incorporating the usual grid of wide streets (named after famous English or Colonial personalities) and a sawmill, magistrate's house, police station and steamboat pier—all focussing on Argyle Square with its adjacent Anglican Church reserve. In June 1860 Bishop Hills and

Rev. James Gammage laid plans for St. Mark's Church on this site.

Designed by Capt. John Grant of the Royal Engineers, it was apparently a replica of Christ Church, Hope, which was constructed one year earlier. As such, it would have displayed the Royal Engineers' direct, carpenter-like approach to detail and decoration, and their concern for the honest expression of materials and structure. Consecration took place on 18 May 1862, and Bishop Hills describes the moment:

... every seat was filled and some stood. There were 59 present, besides about 25 Indians. There were many miners. . . . Very few people of the place were present. They are engrossed in business [for] Sunday is as busy a day as others. Stores are open, wagons are plying, mules are packing exactly as on other days. No one thinks of putting on a different dress. The magistrate was not present. Such are the difficulties with which our clergy have to deal. . . .

After 1864 virtually all activity in Port Douglas ended. In 1873 St. Mark's was dismantled and floated down Harrison Lake on six large Indian canoes, then transported to Chilliwack where it was renamed St. Thomas. Here it remained in constant use until torn down in 1897.

Twenty miles north of Douglas, up the surging Lillooet River, lies the Indian village of Skookumchuck. Once an important stopping point on the wagon trail, close to the bathing waters of St. Agnes Hot Springs, Skookumchuck in the early 1900s was the centre of all festive activities for over four hundred Harrison-Pemberton Indians. Today, only six band members remain and the village consists of a few log and frame houses, a ceremonial hall, and the most outstanding church in the region.

The Roman Catholic Church of the Holy Cross at Skookumchuck is a masterpiece of hand-crafted folk art. Its three prominent spires, the central of which is taken to symbolize Christ, have earned it the alternative name, the Church of the Two Thieves. Because of its isolated position, the building still stands, providing dramatic evidence of the lost splendour of its sister church at Pemberton (Mount Currie).

The church, measuring 25' x 70', rests on large hand-hewn timbers set on great stone footings pulled up from the river. It boasts the richest and most elaborate interior in the diocese. All is handcarved: the priest's chair, the confessionals, the pews, as well as the tabernacle and side altars, which are painted white and trimmed with gold. Its stained-glass side lights and the brilliant rose window cast vibrant patterns on the white clapboard walls and undulating ceiling. The altars dominate the sanctuary—a dazzling display of niches, canopies and flat pinnacles, crock-

eted and topped with trefoil finials and crosses in true Gothic splendour. The delicate curved altar railing and the open latticework of the confessional complement and complete this exuberant display. The Church of the Two Thieves, although late in construction, represents the culmination of a well-tutored folk art tradition in the area.

Not surprisingly, this vernacular, born within the church, finds its final and most sensitive form in the burial grounds of its originators. Their wooden markers, of exquisite beauty, stand side by side in the graveyard at Skookumchuck. Weathered with age, they display simply the names of the deceased and some primitive and touching symbols of spiritual love.

On the Sweeteen Reserve, a few miles north of Skookumchuck, is a mortuary gate carved in cedar in 1910. Gothic and flamboyant, it is a fine example of the intermingling of imported styles and the exuberant, freewheeling use of decoration and relief essentially Indian in nature.

At the head of Lillooet Lake lie the fertile valley and meadows of Pemberton. Port Pemberton, consisting of "a couple of restaurants and a half a dozen huts," has long since vanished. Here, wagon trains and determined men departed for Summit Lake and the final journey by steamboat down Anderson and Seton lakes to Lillooet on the Fraser. Bishop Hills describes part of his journey, beginning with Thursday, 6 June 1861:

After camping at the Summit Lake, we descended from the dividing ridge of the Cascade Range, towards Lake Anderson, which we reached about twelve. The scenery is grand and varied; the valley somewhat widens. We encamped at the head of the lake, which stretches far away in a beautiful placid expanse of blue water, from which rise up the precipitous sides of pine-clad, snow-capped mountains. The lake is about eighteen miles long, and winds amongst the mountains, which break into view, in varied and pleasing continuations.

At seven, we held service at the house at the head of the lake. Mr. Gammage read the Litany; Mr. Garrett and myself preached from Matt. vi:20 and 2 Cor. ix:15. All in the house, and packers and travellers, attended, amongst them a Mexican—all attentive. There were Indians also present.

Catholic missionaries were already at work in the area, as Hills noted on this journey to Seton Portage, but the Roman Catholic church, built here by the Indians of the Necait band, was constructed only in 1895. Now abandoned, this unimposing structure contains one of the most elaborate and original hand-carved altars in the province. This amazing assemblage of religious motifs in blue, white and gold seems distinctively Indian in concept, though

Text continues on page 105

Above & preceding page: THE CHURCH OF ST. MARY, SCOWLITZ

CHURCH OF THE HOLY CROSS, SKOOKUMCHUCK

CHURCH OF THE HOLY CROSS, SKOOKUMCHUCK

GRAVEYARD, SKOOKUMCHUCK

CEMETERY GATE, SWEETEEN RESERVE

Following page: NECAIT CHURCH ALTAR & REREDOS

composed of Gothic design elements such as finials, crockets, quatrefoil panels and variations on the fleur de lis, all displayed in a series of enriched flat surfaces. The altar frieze is especially well executed, featuring a series of fluted ovals supported by two arcarded doorways. At its base a central scallop shell, the emblem of St. James, is contained by an arch or lunette. At altar level an elaborate tabernacle interrupts the corbelled architrave once used for candelabra and the display of flowers. Above it, a large niche, which would traditionally contain the motif of the sacred heart, is flanked by an entablature of flat columns. This recess is crowned by a golden nimbus or crescent, a device used elsewhere in the altarpiece. The altar and screen at Necait well represent the high order of folk art prevalent in the Indian churches of this area.

The fast-flowing Seton River slices through the narrow canyon linking Anderson and Seton lakes and drops 60 feet in 1.5 miles. The barging of supplies between the two bodies of water in 1859 was extremely hazardous, and Lieutenant Palmer, R.E., who had considered a new canal and locks, recommended the installation of a tramway. Two years later, a narrow gauge railway was ingeniously constructed using a track of wood rails and large-wheeled freight wagons hauled by mules. Close to where this tramway ended, at Flushing on Seton Lake, the small log Church of St. Mary still stands, unused and filled with hay. Most of the people of the Slosh band, who at one time actively farmed, freighted and packed with horses to the mines at Bridge River, have quietly left their church and village, drawn to the large work centres. The structure remains, a reminder of life past, its emptiness tempered by the timber walls, a proud and decorative clocher and the remnants of a simple but expressive wood interior.

One mile separates Seton Lake and Lillooet where the gold rush route rejoins the Fraser. Along the way, the small log church of the Cayoosh Creek band, its date and denomination unknown, stands weathered and defiantly erect.

After urgings by Governor Douglas and Bishop Hills to establish a permanent town and erect a church, Colonel Moody of the Royal Engineers granted four lots at the head of the main street of Lillooet to the Church of England, and by Christmas of 1861 the first services were held in the small wooden Church of St. Mary the Virgin. The building was consecrated on 14 September 1862 by Bishop Hills, who noted that the east and west windows were still incomplete but that the church was "certainly an ornament to the place." The Reverend R.C. Lundin Brown and his parishioners had worked hard and contributed much to its $4,274 cost. The clergy subsequently solicited donations from Governor Douglas, Bishop Hills and Lady Burdett-Coutts, who, besides sending cash, provided the altar service, vestments, candelabra, the church bell and a portable melodeon which was shipped around the Horn and packed to Lillooet over the Douglas Trail. The simple white church with its latticed bell cot and delicate windows was built of whipsawn lumber, and the structure with its hand-dressed rafters was held together by wooden pegs. Imported black walnut was used for the pews and the communion rails.

St. Mary's was the fourth oldest church erected in the new mainland colony of British Columbia, after St. John's, Derby; Holy Trinity, New Westminster; and Christ Church, Hope; and it was an important addition to the chain of Anglican missions that linked Victoria to the miners at Barkerville on Williams Creek.

The Church of St. Mary (1860) at Lillooet (PABC)

Sad to say, this historic church was demolished in the 1960s in favour of a new building. All that remains are some furnishings retained in the local museum and remnants of the entry porch lying abandoned in a nearby field.

Three Indian villages above Lillooet—Bridge River, Fountain and Pavilion—were important freighting and supply centres in the days of the Cariboo and Kamloops rush. At the turn of the century, single-tower Gothic churches stood proudly among numerous log houses. Only Holy Trinity at Pavilion still stands. It boasts a tall, square entry tower, a crenelated lantern (that is, the tower superstructure), and a shingled flèche, and commands a central position in the village. At Bridge River on the old Hoystein Reserve, a great white cross marks the cemetery and the weathered grave monuments which are inscribed in the Indian syllabic script—the "Wawa"—devised by Father J.M. Le Jeune.

Twelve miles north, high above the village of Pavilion, lie the great ranch lands of the Pavilion Plateau, one mile

THE CHURCH OF ST. MARY, SETON LAKE

CEMETERY AT THE ABANDONED HOYSTEIN VILLAGE, BRIDGE RIVER

above sea level. Here, the original Cariboo Road winds up the south flank, crosses luxuriant grazing lands and zigzags down to Kelly Lake, Clinton, and the Cariboo beyond.

Many of the early pioneers who came to work the gold fields turned to farming and cattle raising. A few, such as Clement and Henry Cornwall, saw an opportunity to establish large land holdings and take full advantage of the development of the country. In 1862 the Cornwall brothers settled on the bunch grass flats close to where the Bonaparte empties into the Thompson River. They immediately pre-empted 160 acres, planted vegetables and hay, and began stocking horses, mules and oxen. After constructing a sawmill, they erected Ashcroft Manor—an inn and public house on the new Cariboo Road. Then they turned to building a grist mill and establishing one of the largest cattle ranches in the colony. In time, their "estate" covered 6,452 acres.

The Cornwalls lived the life of English aristocracy, enjoying their version of the fox hunt—a coyote was substituted—and entertaining the horsemen of England and the colony at their own race track. The local Indians harvested the crops and acted as cowboys on the ranch.

In 1899 the Indian Agency reported that a "very neat church of hewn logs"—St. John at the Latin Gate, Anglican — had been built here, on Indian land, behind the old manor house. It was furnished inside with dressed lumber and adorned with a classic doorway. The once fertile range of pasture lands which surrounded the edifice is now desert-like, the bunch grass depleted through overgrazing and neglect.

Ten miles farther north the white-painted Roman Catholic church at Bonaparte dominates the modern houses of the village, much as it must have when it was first constructed, just after 1900. Its awkward exterior proportions give little hint of the splendid barrel vault within and its extraordinary painted aureola.

At the confluence of Hat Creek and the Bonaparte River is McLean's Station, which served travellers on the Lillooet–Pavilion route as well as those moving up the new wagon road from the Cornwall ranch. Early missionaries often preached at these and other such stopping places. Bishop Hills was here in June of 1861, and he wrote of the occasion:

We delayed going... for it enabled me to have a service at the station. Two pack trains came in and we had a small but interesting congregation. All the children of Mr. McLean are from Indian mothers. The younger boys are fine children but wild as colts. I saw one six years old lassoing an unbroken raging horse and then mounting it.

Hills was watching the sons of H.B.C. Chief Trader Donald McLean, three of whom later made themselves famous by terrorizing settlers in the Kamloops area and finally killed Constable John Ussher at Nicola in 1879. After a wild shootout at Douglas Lake, all three were captured. They were hanged at New Westminster on 31 January 1881.

Other farms sprouted along the wagon route wherever fertile land could be found. The Indians of the area usually built new villages close to the plantings and soon were erecting log churches of the faith of those who came to minister. Such was the case at Canoe Creek and Dog Creek, and at Alkali Lake, where today a few of the great ranches are still actively producing. The Roman Catholic Church of St. Theresa of the Child Jesus at Canoe Creek is still in use.

Still farther north, on the Sugarcane Indian reserve at the edge of Williams Lake is the Church of the Immaculate Conception, its roof flaring at the edges and its log superstructure clad in a variety of clapboard patterns. Gothic in style, with a substantial tower and rustication, it nonetheless reflects in many ways its Quebec parish church origins. The vaulted roof is a Quebecois feature, and so are the arcaded board and batten panelling on the interior walls and the two rose windows of pure red, yellow and blue glass which enrich and punctuate the space.

The local Indian Agent, E. Bell, in his report of 1899, summarized conditions on the reserve at the time.

The population is 138. The Indians were visited by an epidemic of measles during the spring and a couple of children died from its effects. Otherwise their general health has been good. [Their occupations are] principally farming, teaming their produce to the mines, working as farm hands, ... hunting, fishing and trapping. They have horses, cattle, wagons, sleighs, harnesses, saddles and a good supply of farming implements of all kinds. Quite a number [of children] attend the Williams Lake Industrial School [St. Joseph's Mission]. The women ... manufacture gloves, mitts, moccasins and other wearing apparel from tanned deer-skins .... These Indians all belong to the Roman Catholic Church. They have a very fine building where divine service is regularly held.

After passing 150 Mile House, near Williams Lake, travellers to the mines had to decide either to board the stern-wheeler *Enterprise* at Soda Creek and journey to Williams Creek via Quesnel City and Cottonwood, or to follow the original route to the gold fields by 158 Mile House, Beaver Creek, and Quesnel Forks at the confluence of the Quesnel and Cariboo rivers. Today, the Forks lies abandoned, the finest ghost town in the province.

In 1869 the Yorkshireman Rev. James Reynard, estab-

Text continues on page 118

THE CHURCH OF ST. THERESA OF THE CHILD JESUS, CANOE CREEK

III

THE CHURCH OF ST. JOHN AT THE LATIN GATE, CORNWALL

BONAPARTE: THE ALTAR & THE CEMETERY GATE

CHURCH OF THE IMMACULATE CONCEPTION, SUGARCANE
Opposite: JOSS HOUSE, QUESNEL FORKS

lishing his own church at Barkerville, requested "a missionary...for the Chinamen at the Forks of Quesnelle, numbering nearly 3,000." None came, and the Chinese, who happily reworked the abandoned claims of earlier prospectors, built a joss house instead. It still stands, the beams covered in Chinese script and wallpaper hanging in tatters from the hand-hewn walls.

†

THE BANK OF BRITISH COLUMBIA
Gold dust & bars purchased

Steamer "ENTERPRISE"
at daylight leaves Quesnel for Soda Creek

GAZELLE SALOON
Adler & Barry, Prop'rs.
This large SALOON is fitted up in a style
of elegance and comfort which has no
rival in these colonies.
The bar is furnished with
LIQUORS & SEGARS
of the finest quality & best brands

BARNARD'S EXPRESS
for Lillooet & Yale —
conveying treasure, letters & valuables for
ALL PARTS OF THE WORLD

When these advertisements appeared in the *Cariboo Sentinel*, the booming mining community of Barkerville was billed as the largest city west of Chicago and north of San Francisco. Williams Creek, which supported Barkerville and two other rustic towns—Richfield and Camerontown—was known in 1865 as the richest stream in the world. Miners, shopkeepers, suppliers, and "hurdy-gurdy damsels" poured into the thriving area, and with them came the missionaries seeking to minister and reform.

In the summer of 1862, Bishop Hills led the Anglican Mission to the mines at Lightning, Antler and Williams creeks. He deplored the plight of the miners when he encountered two wagon trains

whose principal cargo was champagne for the mines .... Spirituous liquors have been found in abundance and now the successful miner must be tempted to sink his gains in the works of Champagne—such is mining.

Other men of the cloth followed, including Rev. James Sheepshanks, who for $1,200 built a church in the gold fields—"a small substantial well-proportioned building,"

Hills called it—and Father Magoggin, who bought a house and held services there in 1867. The next year, Bishop D'Herbomez dedicated the hall and bell of St. Patrick's Catholic Church at Richfield. At Barkerville, Rev. Reynard purchased an old building for use as an Anglican Church on Sunday and as a school building throughout the week. Methodists and Presbyterians came, building simple churches and halls, and providing educational and recreational programs as well as religious services. Reynard's activities included operating a lending library and offering religious studies, readings of the classics, band and choir practice, and occasional chess games. To further lure the unruly miners through his doors, he provided public lectures and lantern slides. Reynard and his "Church Institute," patterned after the Mechanics' Institutes of England, provided a challenging alternative to the theatres, saloons and bawdy houses of the day.

On 16 September 1868, a miner trying to kiss one of the dancing girls in the backroom of Adler's and Barry's Saloon displaced the red hot stove pipe that vented through the canvas ceiling and roof. In less than two hours, all of Barkerville was in flames. All was lost—drinking establishments as well as the houses of worship.

A new town arose, different from the first in both content and appearance. Houses and buildings were erected in symmetrical order, the main street was widened, and the raised wooden sidewalks were fixed at a regular and uniform grade in order to avoid the annual flooding of Williams Creek. Only permanent businesses were able to rebuild, for those who had sought quick profits were unable to raise the funds to construct new buildings. Rev. Reynard, who with his family had struggled to survive the winter season, was anxious to join in.

At length, we opened ground for the new church—St. Saviour's .... This lot is at the lower end of the town at the fork of two roads and has a large wedge-shaped plot of vacant ground in front, which I hope to fence in and plant with fir trees. I had spent many a pleasant hour... drawing plans for this church, modest indeed and unpretending, yet decorous in arrangement and effective by mere proportion.

Reynard built his little Gothic church almost single-handedly. He was well aware of "the True Principles of Medieval Architecture" ("the ornamenting of construction—not constructing ornament," as Pugin expressed it), and he relied for architectural effect on bold, simple, well-proportioned forms and spaces, rustication, and a minimum of decoration. Tall windows emphasize the narrow form of the curved chancel and the vertical proportions of the steep-roofed nave. Within, a beautifully crafted archway frames the choir and sanctuary. The building is clad with

14-inch-wide pine boards and 3-inch battens and is held together with square nails. Reynard designed and helped carve many of the decorative arch corbels, vestry furnishings and the pews of spruce wood.

The first service at St. Saviour's was held on 24 September 1870. Rev. Reynard, his health failing, moved soon afterward to Nanaimo, then to Victoria, and died five years later, still a young man. His major achievement, the Church of St. Saviour's, remains in use today, served by the rector of Quesnel.

Many of those for whom Reynard built—to prove, he said "that men working underground have still some hopes which go upward and heavenward"—are buried in the old cemetery above the town. Here lie John "Cariboo" Cameron, who struck it rich shortly after Bill Barker's original strike on Williams Creek; Capt. O.B. Travaillot of the Royal Engineers, one of the first B.C. Land Surveyors in the district; Chartres Brew, the Irishman who was both Chief Gold Commissioner and Chief Inspector of Police; and numerous miners who fell victim to the −40°F temperatures, cave-ins, and typhoid. Their wooden memorials, like Reynard's monument in the town below, are testimonials to the perseverance and courage of the men who lived and struggled in those hectic years.

†

A later and even larger gold rush, to the Klondike in 1897, led to the construction of British Columbia's most northerly place of worship—St. Andrew's Church at Bennett Lake, 47 miles above Skagway, Alaska, and 550 miles from the gold city of Dawson, Yukon Territory.

When George Carmack and his companions struck gold on Bonanza Creek in 1896, news of their discovery caused a mass exodus of would-be miners from San Francisco, Portland, Seattle and Vancouver. With them came the Presbyterian clergy: Rev. Robert M. Dickey, who established a multidenominational church at Skagway, and Andrew S. Grant, who one year later established a log and tent "chapel" at Lake Bennett to serve over a thousand hopefuls awaiting the spring thaw and the long journey down the lakes and the Yukon River to Dawson City. His successor, Rev. John A. Sinclair, born in Ontario and educated at Queens University, was stationed briefly in Skagway, then in 1899 crossed the White Pass for Lake Bennett. For months he commuted between the two centres, ministering as he travelled to construction workers building the new White Pass and Yukon railway connecting Skagway and Whitehorse. At Bennett, he found hundreds of men camped in tents, whipsawing lumber and building plank and resin-seamed barges, rafts, and canvas boats for the journey north. A year earlier, over ten thousand had wintered here and, after the ice break-up in late May, over seven thousand boats and floating craft of all descriptions started down the lake to the gold fields. Rev. Sinclair was determined to build a substantial church at Bennett City and, with volunteer carpenters awaiting the spring thaw, started construction on St. Andrew's.

Capt. John Irving, of Fraser River steamboat fame and a member of the provincial government, gave the address at the laying of the cornerstone. He paid tribute to the "energetic pioneers" such as Rev. Sinclair and noted that piles of discarded spruce slabs not used for boat building had been gathered and applied as "a distinctive artistic patterned exterior for the church." Windows of leaded glass were provided as a gift from St. Andrew's in Vancouver, and the Victoria church of the same name lent a small organ. Interior

St. Andrew's Church, at Lake Bennett (YA)

walls were finished in cedar, and eventually hanging lamps, hand-carved pews and an altar were installed. Sinclair was pleased:

Our pretty little church is the most popular rendezvous in town. Our people hold social evenings, write letters, have business meetings, meet engagements, read, smoke, even file saws and sometimes do a little courting in the place which, in a more conventional town, would be reserved exclusively for worship.

Then abruptly, in September 1900, St. Andrew's closed. The White Pass and Yukon railway was completed to Whitehorse, the riverboats moved away and the city at the end of Bennett Lake was abandoned. Only Rev. Sinclair's rustic church remains today, a lonely survivor of the greatest gold rush North America has ever seen.

ST. SAVIOUR'S, BARKERVILLE

CEMETERY, BARKERVILLE
Opposite: ST. SAVIOUR'S

The Great Conversion

Stikine
Peace
Aiyansh
Nass
Kispiox
Hagwilget
Kincolith
Kitwanga
Kitseguecla
Cedarvale
Port Simpson
Skeena
Metlakatla
Yan
Masset
Fraser
Columbia
Thompson
Alert Bay
Lytton
Nicola
Spahomin
Kelowna
Fort Steele
St. Eugene
Hesquiat
Sechelt
Ustlawn
Yale
Hope
Moyie
Mission City
Cowichan
© 1980 ROBERT BRINGHURST LTD.

Preceding pages: BLACKFISH POLE & THE CHURCH OF ST. MARY MAGDALENE, HAGWILGET;
REV. J.B MC CULLAGH LAYING THE LOG FOUNDATION FOR THE CHURCH OF THE HOLY TRINITY, AIYANSH (PABC)

By THE LATE 1860s, ALL MAJOR CHRISTIAN DENOMINATIONS were active on Vancouver Island and the mainland. They competed with one another, seeking to attract the largest congregations and to build the first churches in new colonial communities and among isolated bands of native Indians. For the aboriginals, the great conversion was on. All denominations felt themselves hard pressed and were constantly requesting additional clergy from their Canadian and European societies and orders.

And they came. By 1863, eleven Catholic priests served the missions of the Pacific on Vancouver Island, under Bishop Demers, and on the mainland under the jurisdiction of Bishop D'Herbomez. Dedicated Anglican clergy and lay preachers came from the religious colleges of Cambridge, Oxford, Canterbury and Dublin, to organize both white and Indian congregations. Later, in 1879, the Anglican ecclesiastical territory of Vancouver Island and British Columbia, initially governed by Bishop Hills, was divided into three geographic sections. Hills presided over the Vancouver Island Diocese of Columbia, Rev. Acton W. Sillitoe was appointed Bishop of the southern part of British Columbia, the Diocese of New Westminster, and the Right Reverend William Ridley assumed responsibility for the northern section, the Diocese of Caledonia. The Methodists, who arrived in Victoria in 1859, were soon ministering to the white and Indian peoples of Nanaimo, Chilliwack, Bella Bella, Kitimat, Fort Simpson and the villages of the Skeena and Nass rivers. Presbyterians, funded by the Church of Scotland, continued their work in Victoria and spread out to serve mostly Protestant settlers in Nanaimo, Comox, Alberni, Langley and the Nicola Valley. The Baptists arrived in Victoria in 1877, erecting a church on Pandora Street, and later became active in New Westminster, Nanaimo and in the busy sawmill town of Vancouver.

For those missionaries determined to impart their faith to the native Indians of the coast and interior, the task became ever more challenging. Entire villages were threatened by smallpox and with other diseases introduced by Europeans and North Americans, and the evangelists were forced to serve as medics, vaccinating the endangered and burying the dead. The degenerative influence of white settlement and trade, and a desire on the part of the missionaries to change the secular as well as the spiritual lives of the Indians, caused the establishment of self-sufficient model villages and the construction of large mission schools. The native peoples' love for pageantry, music and dance was not overlooked, and festivals and brass bands were organized, so that by the late 1880s most missions had advanced, as Father Morice said, "to the more elaborate stage of the medieval church, with her beautiful ceremonies and her religious plays or mysteries."

By the turn of the century, the conversion was nearly absolute. Much had been irretrievably lost—old beliefs and rituals, old ways of life and culture never again to be experienced. During this period, which was both evolutionary and destructive, some of the province's finest churches were erected. Most were spontaneous and joyous expressions of a spiritual love nurtured by zealous apostolics determined to achieve a common goal—the transformation and sanctification of heathen life.

Although William Duncan of the Anglican Church Missionary Society was early at work among the Tsimshian, it was the Catholic Church which first established permanent missions and schools for the Indians of the lower North Pacific Coast. In 1858, Father Peter Rondeault requested a posting in the Cowichan Valley and had erected a wooden church and house on Comiaken Hill, overlooking the village longhouses and the bay beyond. Matthew Macfie, whose book *Vancouver Island and British Columbia* was published in 1865, describes the mission station.

Arriving at Cowitchin one summer evening about eight o'clock, in a canoe, after a long day's paddling, I heard the sound of chanting proceeding from the native church, which was erected and supplied with altar furniture chiefly, if not entirely, at the expense of the Indians. It was a log structure about 50 feet by 20 and on a high situation.... On entering the church I observed a frère engaged in teaching some Indian lads hymns used in devotional exercises, which they sang with taste and vigour.

The church, dedicated to St. Ann, held over four hundred worshippers, and served the Somenos, Quamichan, Comiaken and Clemclemaluts for ten years until the erection of a stone church immediately adjacent. This second church was built chiefly by Father Rondeault himself, Chief Joe Tazlpaymoult, four Indian helpers, and William Williams, a stonemason from Victoria. The good Father was determined to have a permanent church and sold butter produced on his farm in order to pay the $500 masonry fee. The sandstone used was quarried from the site. It was broken up, it is said, by Joe Tazlpaymoult, who employed an old cannon ball shot into the village years before by one of Governor Douglas's ships of the line, the H.M.S. *Thetis*.

The new St. Ann's, known for many years as the "Butter Church," was consecrated in 1870 by Bishop Demers. It is 30 feet wide by 64 feet long and has solid walls of stone 2 feet thick. Mass was held regularly and the church was the scene of many festivals and processionals which included the Indian girls from the nearby Convent of St. Ann.

Concern about the religious, moral and domestic

training of future mothers of the surrounding tribes prompted the Sisters of St. Ann in Victoria to open a boarding school in Quamichan. In 1862, Sister Mary Ellen McTucker and Father Rondeault preempted four hundred acres for a new school and, in so doing, were among the first settlers in the Cowichan District. Two years later, with help from pioneer farmers, a log school was erected. Sister Mary of the Sacred Heart and Sister Mary Conception arrived to take charge, having brought with them from Victoria only their personal belongings and a cow, a gift from an ex-miner. There were no beds, and the first school children slept on woven mats on the floor. Furniture was made as it was required, and soon a well-tended farm supplied meat, vegetables and Father Rondeault's butter. Ten

The "Butter Church" at Cowichan (PABC)

years after its construction, the stone church was abandoned in favour of another St. Ann's, a frame structure which still stands close to the residential school, two miles away.

The mission farmlands are now overgrown, and the priest's residence and convent are no longer used, but within the third Church of St. Ann's at Cowichan can be found the remnants of another era, including a baptismal font dedicated to Father Rondeault, and a finely carved Gothic altar set proudly in a simple arched sanctuary.

Of the Indian missions established by the colonists and their clergy on Vancouver Island, none was more representative of the diligence, hard work and courage of the missionaries than that founded at Hesquiat by Father Augustus Joseph Brabant. Hesquiat became the centre of religious activity on the rugged wind-swept west coast, and its hardy priest served the main villages of the Central and Northern Nootkan tribes for thirty-four years. During his first visits to the area in the company of Demers's succes-

sor, Bishop Charles Seghers, Brabant found the Indians indifferent to his ministrations. At Tahsis, for instance,

we found these Indians in full glee—a dead whale had drifted on their land and the houses were full of blubber, which the women were boiling and reducing to oil. I do not think that anything that we could have said under the circumstances would have had much effect. . . .

Of all the tribes visited, the Hesquiats seemed the most friendly, and in 1875 Father Brabant, with Father Rondeault of Quamichan, was ordered to establish a permanent mission in their village. The Fathers took along three calves, one bull and two heifers which were destined to become the pioneer cattle on the west coast of the island.

In the preceding year, the bark *Edwin*, loaded with lumber, had split open off Estevan Point and the Indians had rescued many of the sailors from the heavy surf. The ship had washed up on the beach, and from the remaining lumber and decking Father Brabant and his converts built their first church.

Left alone at the new mission, Brabant began to study the Nootkan language, and soon managed to teach the tribe the Catholic Ladder. Within a year, however, the dreaded smallpox had decimated the village, striking down the daughter of Chief Matlahaw. Although vaccinated by Brabant, Matlahaw became obsessed with fear and in a rage shot the priest in the hand and back. For days Brabant lay in his house, fainting periodically as the Indians threw cold water over his inflamed wounds. After he had prepared himself for death and lapsed into delirium a British man-of-war entered the harbour. The next day he was carried on board the H.M.S. *Rocket* and taken to Victoria where he remained under the care of the Sisters of St. Ann for five months. Courageously he returned to Hesquiat, to be greeted warmly and feted by the Indians. His assailant had died of exposure in the dense forest close to the village.

Brabant established a force of resident "policemen," giving them a coat and pants as a mark of their authority. He also taught the Hesquiats to sing and before long held the first High Mass. On 1 October 1875, he and Bishop Seghers placed the little 26' x 60' church under the patronage of St. Antoine. In attendance were the neighbouring Muchalat, Clayoquot and Ahousat Nootka, who were soon to have churches of their own.

Father Brabant was both architect and builder, doing much of the carpentry work himself. He built churches at Sarita for the Ohiet, at Ahousat, and at Friendly Cove for the Moachat. In 1891, he constructed the second church at Hesquiat, aided by two French Canadian carpenters. This time the plan was drawn by Stephen Donovan of Victoria, in a style reminiscent of a Quebec parish church. Today a

THE THIRD CHURCH OF ST. ANN, COWICHAN

THE SECOND CHURCH OF ST. ANN — THE BUTTER CHURCH — AT COWICHAN

CHURCH OF ST. ANTOINE, HESQUIAT (PHOTO BY HENRY HAWTHORN)

OUR LADY OF LOURDES, SECHELT

modern sanctuary remains. As before, a long boardwalk leads from the beach across a marshy thicket to a little church of weathered wood set deeply in the forest.

Of all the wooden churches built on Vancouver Island, Christ Church on Cormorant Island is the most ornate and Victorian in style. It stands at the water's edge, a picturesque version of several Gothic-revival predecessors, displaying its sawtooth trim, simulated stone coining, decorative roof comb and airy bell cot. Colour highlights these embellishments in keeping with New York architect George Woodward's dictum of 1865 that the "projecting and ornamental parts [should be painted] two or three shades darker than the body of the building. This will give a depth of shadow and expression which cannot be obtained in any other way."

Christ Church was erected by Rev. A.J. Hall, who was first sent to Fort Rupert by the Church Missionary Society in 1878 and to Alert Bay a year later. Here he ministered to the Nimpkish for thirty-three years, establishing a mission, school and hospital which served the surrounding villagers at Blunden Harbour, Hope Island, Kingcome Inlet, Turnour Island, New Vancouver, Village Island, Fort Rupert and Deserter Island. Hall concentrated on learning the native language and translated the gospels into the Kwakwalla tongue over a period of years. He believed in practising the full gospel, emphasizing evangelism, education and effective living. In 1887 he constructed a steam-driven sawmill in the village "affording a good deal of employment," as he said, producing "lumber shipped to Victoria for biscuit boxes [and] cordwood for the cannery and steamers." Five years later, Hall erected Christ Church, offering services in Kwakwalla in the morning and English in the evening. Today, inside the building one can find a large stained-glass window commemorating the ministry of Rev. Hall and other modern windows, by Sointula artist Larry Sommer, dedicated to the missionary's wife Elizabeth and to pioneer church members from the Stephen Cook family. Arches supporting the roof are cut from 18-inch wood planks spliced and joined with dowels. Their graceful forms recall the stone vaults of another age.

On the mainland, some 160 miles southeast of Cormorant Island, an empty field at the sea's edge marks the former location of Our Lady of Lourdes, the fourth Roman Catholic church to be built on the Sechelt reserve. From 1902 until 1970, when it burned to the ground, the great white wooden church with the magnificent tower served as a beacon to village fishermen and others sailing the Strait of Georgia. Like its predecessor of 1890, the twin-spired Church of Our Lady of the Rosary, it was of fine proportions, resplendent with Romanesque and carpenter-Gothic detail. Both buildings were erected by the villagers

at the behest of Bishop Pierre Paul Durieu, o.m.i. A strict and harsh prelate, he established at Sechelt and at North Vancouver new model communities and a mission system which became famous up and down the coast.

Durieu was born in France in 1830, served as a missionary in the Washington Territory and on Vancouver Island, and in 1875 was consecrated vicar apostolic of British Columbia and coadjutor to Bishop D'Herbomez, whom he eventually succeeded. As vicar apostolic, he toured his missions tirelessly, emphasizing eucharistic devotions, music and ceremony. Father Morice tells us that Durieu established a brass band at Sechelt "with gorgeous uniforms for the players," and that he even procured pieces of cannon with

Bishop Durieu's Church, Sechelt (PABC)

which "to celebrate the arrival of [a] missionary, or enhance the solemnity of the processions of the Blessed Sacrament." In his model village at Sechelt, Indian "watchmen" under the authority of the priests and bishop enforced the Indian Act and the precepts of the Church as well as the by-laws of the village.

The first mass celebrated on the shores of Burrard Inlet was held at Ustlawn, now North Vancouver, in the year 1860. Six years later, a log chapel was raised and when, twenty-four years later, Bishop Durieu sought to amalgamate the tribes of the inlet with those of the Squamish River, Howe Sound and Musqueam, St. Paul's Church was erected. The nave of the present building is that of the original edifice, though it was much remodelled and enlarged in 1909. Its twin Gothic spires now face the busy harbour and city of Vancouver.

At Ustlawn, grand pageants and retreats were held. The Vancouver *News-Advertiser* gave this account of the feast of Corpus Christi in June 1888:

CHRIST CHURCH, ALERT BAY

Following: THE OBLATE CEMETERY AT ST. MARY'S MISSION

The main street was hung with festoons of evergreens mingled with coloured lanterns.... A large canvas tent or tabernacle was erected just back of the church, and a temporary altar raised which, when its many candles were lighted, presented a really beautiful appearance....

The celebration commenced with a solemn service and benediction by His Lordship Bishop Durieu, which was held in the large tabernacle.... The dark rows of kneeling worshippers, the bright altar showing up beautifully in the deepening twilight, the rich vestments of the bishop and attendants all combined to make a picture worthy of the brush of a Rembrant or a Murillo....

After the service was over the Indians proceeded to their canoes, which had been decorated with coloured paper lanterns, and the procession was formed.... There were 154 canoes in the procession, and the effect of the many-coloured lights reflected on the glass-like surface of the

centre of native religious activity in the lower Fraser Valley.

Like so many apostles of the day, Fouquet was his own architect, builder and tenant, erecting rustic palaces of logs and enduring the cold comfort which they afforded.

Three hundred acres of land were purchased for the mission overlooking the Fraser River and Matsqui prairie beyond. In these early years before the coming of the railway, mission buildings were located on the flat sandbanks. Here the first industrial school for boys, a large whitewashed church, a convent for Indian girls, and the priest's house were built.

In the 1880s new buildings were erected on the bluff, and these, like many of the Catholic schools erected in those times, were in the Second Empire style—a seventeenth-century Parisian mode requiring mansard roofs and classic Renaissance details.

The mission church at Ustlawn, North Vancouver, in 1886 (ACV)

water was really fairy-like. Two Indian bands, one from Fort Douglas and the other belonging to the mission, were amongst the procession and played several of the sweet old tunes of the Catholic Church. In the intervals of playing the Indians chanted hymns, the effect over the water being beautiful. The night was all that could be desired: a nearly full moon hung in the cloudless sky, with hardly the shadow of a breeze to ruffle the calm surface of the inlet. After making a circuit of about a couple of miles, the procession returned to the village, being greeted both on its departure and return with a firing of cannon.

Bishop D'Herbomez had only begun to establish Catholic missions among the mainland Indians when, in 1861, the death of his Superior General necessitated his return to France. He appointed Father Léon Fouquet in charge of the Pacific Coast missions, and Fouquet at once set about founding the Mission of St. Mary, at what is now Mission City. In the ensuing years it became the greatest

In 1892, Father Fouquet also erected a shrine in a grotto dedicted to Our Lady of Lourdes. Set in a grassy amphitheatre surrounded by tall trees, it was the object of further processionals, and as late as 1941 this holy place attracted over five thousand pilgrims. Now only the untended fields remain, and the foundations of the old structures are concealed in wild grass. In the cemetery adjacent can be found the graves of most of the famous evangelists of the Order of Mary Immaculate—Bishop D'Herbomez, Father Fouquet, and many others who spent their lives among the Indians of their missions.

During his long service among the native peoples of British Columbia, Father Fouquet worked not only at St. Mary's Mission. In 1873, he and Brother John Burns set out for the land of the Kootenay Indians, in the western foothills of the Rocky Mountains. They found here a wild and unproductive terrain, inhabited by a nomadic people who crossed the continental divide to hunt the buffalo of the great plains, then returned each year to fish and harvest

roots and berries in the Columbia watershed and the Tobacco Plains. The energetic priests set to work clearing land, seeding wheat, and building a flour mill, log church and hospital. As the great buffalo herds diminished in the 1880s, depleted through massive hunting, the Kootenay ceased to roam and were encouraged to establish a permanent residence at St. Eugene. Father Fouquet served their needs for fourteen years until relieved in 1887 by Father Nicholas Coccola, o.m.i., who transformed the mission and built churches throughout the district.

Father Coccola was dismayed by the undeveloped and impoverished state of St. Eugene Mission, and he pressed his villagers to seek out the precious ore which so many others had discovered in the area. In 1893 an Indian named Pierre found a large galena deposit, rich in silver and lead, on a bluff above Moyie Lake. Two claims were staked and the St. Eugene Mining Company was established. From the sale of shares in the operation, Pierre was able to build a grand house and Father Coccola to build two churches — St. Eugene, on the mission flats at the edge of the St. Mary River, and St. Peter's, on the hill at Moyie. Fine detail and excellence of design mark both, but the standard of finish and the quality of workmanship at St. Eugene remain unexcelled in early Romanist building. In the softly formed, well-composed interior, varied clapboard panels are contained within pine wood trim, accentuated by dark brown paint to further dramatize the linear delights of the surface. Rich stained-glass windows illuminate the nave, and at the altar a beautifully constructed tabernacle punctuates the sanctuary. Outside, decorative shingle scallops, repetitive pinnacles, trefoils, gablet-like birdhouses and ornate metal crosses culminate in a spire soaring to the heavens.

Father Coccola's bonanza church of St. Peter's, built in 1901, still stands in the quiet town of Moyie on the east bank of Moyie Lake. Rock spillage from the old mine workings on the hill behind has taken on a new growth of timber, and at the south end of town, slag heaps stretch along the highway and tumble into the lake. The interior of St. Peter's is today much as it was during those years when the mines and town were thriving. Walls are finished in a white plaster, and two fluted columns highlighted in gold support the sanctuary vault. Old decorative glass lanterns still light the nave of this charming building.

At Fort Steele, nine miles from Cranbrook, Father Coccola was charged with building a third church, St. Anthony's, to service a thriving community — a result of new activity at the North Star mine near present-day Kimberley. Here the pine wood church constructed in 1897 stands next to its Presbyterian neighbour, less than a block from the old schoolhouse on Rocky Mountain Avenue,

which three years earlier served all denominations in the village — Catholics, Anglicans and Presbyterians.

The first missionaries in the Okanagan district, however, were Father Charles M. Pandosy and Father Pierre Richard, both members of the Order of Mary Immaculate who had come via the Oregon country in 1847. In 1859, on the instruction of their superior, Bishop D'Herbomez, they established the Mission of the Immaculate Conception at Mission Creek on the eastern shore of Lake Okanagan. The weathered buildings can be visited today, just south of Kelowna. Sturdy notched log walls contain a small chapel, root cellar and Brothers' residence, all set in what was once part of the old mission farm.

When there were still few places of worship in this valley, devout homesteaders sometimes built their own. Some, such as Quebec-born Cornelius O'Keefe, constructed whole towns complete with general store, post office, sawmill and blacksmith shop. In 1867, O'Keefe, with his friend Thomas Greenhow, drove a herd of cattle from Oregon to the north end of Okanagan Lake. A year later he appropriated 162 acres ten miles above Priests' Valley (the site of present-day Vernon) and began construction of his log house. By 1872 he had built a general store and post office, and fourteen years later, with the help of his neighbours, he built the little Chapel of St. Ann. It was serviced by travelling clergymen, never having its own in residence. The chapel is still there, and a few years ago was opened by O'Keefe's descendants for public viewing.

†

Adjoining Fort Hope is the village of the Tum Sioux Indians. It presents the usual characteristics of an Indian village, but we must not omit to mention that, in addition to these their ordinary habitations, this tribe have a number of holes dug in the earth, which, when roofed over, are intended to form their dwelling-places in very severe weather.

On the occasion of one of my visits to this village, I heard sounds of chanting, in which many voices were mingled, issuing from one of the larger huts, and bearing a striking resemblance in their general character to a Roman Catholic service. My curiosity being aroused, I essayed to enter, but was arrested on the threshold by a functionary in a blanket, who evidently filled the office of a Tum Sioux "Bumble."* After a time, however, I was admitted, and before the service was entirely concluded, I found a party of Indians, to the number of thirty or forty, engaged in

---

* The name of the beadle in Charles Dickens's *Oliver Twist.*

Text continues on page 144

ST. EUGENE

139

ST. EUGENE

MISSION OF THE IMMACULATE CONCEPTION, OKANAGAN LAKE

THE CHAPEL OF ST. ANN, O'KEEFE

bowing and crossing themselves in the intervals of chanting. I did not observe that they made use of any of the emblems of the Romish Church, but feel sure that the atmosphere of the place in which they were assembled would, at any rate, have been greatly improved by the introduction of a little incense.

So wrote Capt. C.E. Barrett-Lennard of Indian religious life at Fort Hope in 1860. Within a year of this famous visit and the publication of his travels in British Columbia, two churches had been built in the little three-street town which surrounded the old Hudson's Bay fort — Father Grandidier's log chapel and Rev. A.D. Pringle's Christ Church. Both denominations served the white community and native Indians of the Coquihalla.

Christ Church, Hope (PABC)

In those hectic days, Hope was a main supply depot for the miners working the Fraser River and the Cariboo. The priests and clergymen establishing residence in the town found it hard going. Not only were they faced with the difficulties and costs of church construction, but the saloon keepers of the town complained openly of "the undue interference of foreigners with their licenced trade."

Remarkably, Christ Church still stands on its original site. Constructed by White & Manson of New Westminster for $1,903 in 1861, it was designed by Capt. John Grant, who served under Colonel Moody of the Royal Engineers.

Bishop Hills befriended Colonel Moody and welcomed his considerable help in the selection of sites and construction of the first mainland churches. In July 1860, Hills discussed with Moody the plan of a church at Hope, and one year later he laid the cornerstone, even though "the roof was already on." In November, a packed house attended the consecration of Christ Church. Townsfolk, Indians and

eighty Royal Engineers were in attendance "and gave a true and hearty character to the proceedings."

At the completion of Christ Church, the New Westminister *British Columbian* devoted an article to the details of its construction:

Built in the Elizabethan [sic] style of architecture, [it is] 50 x 25 feet including chancel and vestry. [The] walls are 12' high and the height from floor to ridge is 28'. The ridge of nave, chancel and porch are finished with an ornamental comb, and the Bell tower on the west end is carried up 14' above the ridge. The windows which are square headed are of diamond sashes. [The] interior . . . is plain, but exceedingly commodious. The walls are all built of plank of equal width planed on the inside, and the joints covered with a planed batten bevelled on the edges. The roof, which is an open one, is also constructed of planed lumber. The Pulpit [is] octagonal of Red wood. The Chancel is enclosed by the Communion rail . . . composed of a series of panels of open gothic work or tracery. . . . In short, Christ Church is a very handsome edifice, and reflecting the greatest credit upon Mr. White, the builder, as well as on the architect.

The little church has mellowed with the years. The board and batten planking has turned to a rich, dark brown, and although structural cross ties and wall supports have been added, the Engineers' fine detailing can still be seen. Remarkable are the thin, chamfered truss members, painted white; the simple hand-cut screens and altar rails in the sanctuary; and the ingenious wood ventilation flaps, located where the walls meet the sloping roof. Handmade diamond glass panes, 10 inches long and full of air bubbles, are still set in the original sash bars. Colour is introduced by the red cedar pulpit and lectern, the flags of the Royal Engineers, and the remnants of a Victorian carpet in the sanctuary — a gift again of Baroness Burdett-Coutts. Christ Church is spartan in design, a product of the direct approach and economy of means sought by the architects of Queen Victoria's military. At the same time, it remains one of the most agreeable and expressive of British Columbia's wooden parish churches, a functional design of great beauty.

By the end of 1862, because of the building of the Cariboo Road, the centre of shipping and commerce had shifted upstream from Hope to Fort Yale at the head of the Great Canyon. The Chinese, some three thousand strong, were reworking the river bars while Canadian, English and American miners sought richer returns in the Cariboo. Rev. William Burton Crickmer, recently of Derby, was the first Anglican missionary in the town. He preached to miners and Indians in a log hut and a converted store until

CHRIST CHURCH, HOPE
Following page: ST. JOHN THE DIVINE, YALE

1863 when his successor, Henry Reeve, arrived to build St. John the Divine on property allocated by Colonel Moody.

St. John the Divine, designed in Victoria by architects Wright & Saunders, served a varied congregation—Royal Engineers (who were surveying and constructing the Cariboo Road), the townspeople, transient miners, Indians and Chinese. Vicar Henry Reeve, who had previously ministered in Shanghai, conversed with the Cantonese merchants and was able to solicit contributions from them for the construction of his church. In the ensuing years, an Indian chapel was erected close to the reserve on the Yale River. It was a flimsy affair—"the snow coming through the roof made it very trying," we are told—and it was replaced by a chapel-school in 1869. Nineteen years later, All Hallows Indian School for Girls was opened in the extensive grounds and former residence of Andrew Onderdonk, the American contractor who built a section of the Canadian Pacific Railway through the hazardous Fraser River Canyon.

Most of Yale's old buildings have disappeared. A native Catholic Church, St. Joseph's, is still used, and St. John the Divine, now refurbished, welcomes its parishioners each week. At the west end of town, close to where Onderdonk's Victorian house stood, can be found the pioneer cemetery. Its few grave markers are lost in the long grass, but from this vantage point one can look down the river across the gravel bars that once teemed with men searching for gold.

†

Lytton Siwashes tum tum mika cloosh hyack chaco. Tikke wawa mika. With this plea in Chinook, five hundred Thompson Indians summoned Rev. John Booth Good to Lytton. Having served in Nanaimo for many years and then in Yale, Good was eager to come. Not only did he wish to evangelize the aboriginals, but he was taken by the challenge of the country as well. His Bishop described the site of the new mission.

*There cannot be a more beautiful and striking spot. On an elevated plateau some 300 feet above the Fraser, about half a mile from the river, are situated the Mission buildings: the Mission-house in a grove of pines (*Pinus ponderosa*) to the left, looking down the church site; in front and to the right the school-house, barn, and catechist's residence. At the back the mountain rises gradually to a height of some 3,000 feet, the sides covered with pines; over the river in front, looking west, a mountain rises some 2,000 feet; down the river to the south is a fine view of water, wood, and mountain, shading into each other; to the north is the mountain which stands in the fork of the Fraser and the Thompson. A stream flows at the back of the house and down to the river, fertilizing the earth as it goes. The whole section belonging to the Mission, or rather which is secured to it, contains about 160 acres. The main road to Cariboo passes through it, and the new church will be a marked object from the road.*

Rev. Good's territory extended from Boston Bar, on the Fraser, to Lillooet, Clinton, Kamloops, and into the Nicola Valley. He served permanent churches at Lytton and Lillooet (St. Mary's the Virgin), visited the Kamloops Station, and had native chapels erected at Boston Bar, Boothroyds, Stryen, Quolsopah's Camp, Ashcroft, Nicola and Cooks

The Church of St. John, Yale (PABC)

Ferry (Spence's Bridge). Most were located on the narrow benches high above the muddy Fraser and the blue-green Thompson. Here, in the Indian encampments, Good ministered inside the keekwillees, the underground pit-houses in which the natives lived during the long cold winters. He followed their migrations, covering great distances, instructing, offering medical assistance, settling differences, conducting burial services and erecting the red cross flag of the church whenever possible. "It will," he said, "be readily understood how very difficult it is to exercise an efficient oversight over a body of Indians so independent and nomadic as ours . . . and so widely scattered throughout so extensive a range of country." Influential he was, however, and proved a hard taskmaster. Acceptance in the church required a certificate of membership in the Anglican mission at Lytton. A complete change of family life was expected. Polygamy was outlawed; monogamous marriage and the baptism of children were enjoined; Sunday worship was mandatory. The applicant was required to learn the catechism, confess before the congregation, and be baptized at a Great Festival (often the occasion of the Bishop's visit). Only then could confirmation and Holy Communion take place. Good's first church, St. Paul's, was a converted tenement painted white and topped at the entry with a small exposed bell. A 15' x 40' log school was built on the same property.

In 1884 Rev. Richard Small succeeded Good, later becoming superintendent of all missions in the diocese—a position he filled until his death in 1909. Sts. Mary and Paul Church, constructed in his time, sits below the native cemetery and a busy highway. Its lich gate, a later addition, offers shade and shelter now as it did when the church-school was the hub of all religious activity in the area.

Indian graveyard at Lytton. Photo by R. Maynard (PABC)

At Shakan in the Nicola Valley, the Gateway to Heaven —and to the old Indian cemetery—is embellished with heraldic decorations and painted a stark white. It contrasts dramatically with the sage and dark green of the pines on the bank behind. Bishop Hills in his diary described an earlier burial ground:

I have passed many Indian burial places. These consist of upright poles—with cross bars upon which are suspended the favourite blanket or portion of dress of the deceased. Blankets red, green, red and blue we frequently saw. These float in the wind above. Beneath are wooden square box-like tombs upon which are carvings. Usually the figure of a man, dressed in Hat, Shirt and Trousers with hands in his pockets is the principal attraction.... The carving is rude, a favourite animal to delineate is the beaver or sometimes a bird... but nowhere have I seen the slightest trace of religious feeling....

Years later, the deceased were interred below ground and

pickets erected. On tall poles a cross was affixed or a red cross flag was mounted and left to flutter in the wind until destroyed by weather and time.

At the west end of Nicola Lake stands the first Presbyterian Church built in the area, St. Andrew's, or the "Murray" Church, named after Rev. George Murray, who enjoyed a roving commission from Yale to Clinton. In 1877, he built his 19' x 27' church at Nicola to serve as his headquarters for the entire district.

The abandoned church of St. Nicholas, at the Indian village of Spahomin near Douglas Lake, is a fine example of Romanist building in the late 1800s. There were earlier log churches in the Nicola district, but active missionaries and devout converts, often enlisting the help of ranchers in the area, soon erected larger frame buildings with steep roofs and prominent towers. Churches of similar proportions at Shulus and Quilchena are still is use.

By the turn of the century, the Indian Agent was able to issue an encouraging report of the Spahomin band, most of whom farmed, raised stock, or worked for others as cowboys on the abundant and magnificent stretches of bunch grass grazing land surrounding the village.

Their buildings, houses and stables are of a superior order, being of logs and frame, larger and better furnished throughout than the majority of Indian houses. [They] are the most extensive stock-raisers in the agency.... Some of the best stallions and brood mares to be found in the province are owned by these Indians. Their cattle are also of a high grade. They are well supplied with farm implements—ploughs, harrows, wagons, sleighs, harness and saddles, mowers, horse-rakes and reaping machines.... All belong to the Roman Catholic denomination. They have two fine churches, and are devout and earnest worshippers.

The San Jose Valley near Williams Lake is one of the most beautiful and fertile in the Cariboo, and it was here that the Oblates founded their fourth major mission and residential school. Established in 1867, St. Joseph's served the white settlers, the Carriers, the Chilcotin and the Shuswap villages on both sides of the Fraser River from Quesnel to Canim Lake. Father James McGuckin selected the site with the intention of building an industrial school for the children of the ranchers and miners in the district. Soon, however, he was encouraging the Indian people to assist him in his newly established cattle ranch.

He built a log chapel, residence and school, and after many years of pleading with his Oblate Superior for teaching and financial help—he considered Bishop D'Herbomez a penny pincher—he was rewarded in 1876 with the arrival of three Sisters of St. Ann from New Westminster. School children came from the entire district, from families

LICH GATE AT THE CHURCH OF STS. MARY & PAUL, LYTTON

THE GATEWAY TO HEAVEN, SHAKAN

ST. ANDREW'S CHURCH, NICOLA

THE CHURCH OF ST. NICHOLAS, SPAHOMIN

whose fathers laboured as farm hands, cowboys or freighters of supplies to the mines. They came having little knowledge of religion and spoke neither English nor French. Yet, within a year, McGuckin said, all were trained to be "obedient, polite and industrious." The good Father continued to be frustrated by problems, however. One severe winter he lost a third of his cattle and horses, and in another found himself unable to collect school fees from wayward miners and from farmers ruined by drought, fire and flood. He soon persuaded the government to pitch in and provide farm acreage for nearby Indian reserves, and by 1882 both the villagers and St. Joseph's itself were in the main self-sufficient. In that year, the 980-acre ranch held only 150 head of cattle and 17 horses.

Father McGuckin travelled farther and farther from his post in an effort to convert the Chilcotin, who still fought intertribal wars and maintained their pagan practices. It was left to Father François Marie Thomas to complete the job when he arrived at St. Joseph's in 1897. This strong, energetic man ministered to white and Indian alike throughout his vast territory, travelling by boat, horseback and sleigh as the occasion demanded. Often suffering from frostbite, and living on a diet of bacon and smoked fish, he served for thirty years, and became the most beloved of all missionaries in the Cariboo.

St. Joseph's is now only partially used. In the early 1950s, the buildings were judged outdated fire traps. They were replaced, and all of the original structures were either burned or demolished. A simple frame school building now sits close to the site of the early church. Behind, near the road, lies the old cemetery, containing the graves of many who laboured here. In the summer evening sun, their markers catch the warm light and meld into one with the long grass meadows and the hills beyond.

†

A weathered totem pole stands majestically across the fields from the Catholic Church of St. Mary Magdalen at the Carrier village of Hagwilget, "the mild people," at the edge of the surging Bulkley River. At one time, the village and its plank longhouses stood in line on a ledge halfway down the precipitous face. The villagers' food was the salmon of the river, and they fished with double-pronged spears or with baskets attached at right angles to long poles set firmly in the rocks. Following the ways of the adjacent Gitksan community, known as the Gitenmaks, or torch-light-fishing-people, they did much of their fishing at night. The villagers of Hagwilget still fish from the gravel bar at the bend in the river below the old site, and their respect for aquatic life is evident in the blackfish emblem

carved above the lower figures in one of their memorial poles. Soft colours highlight symbols representing myths, legends and family history, and contrast dramatically with the white, blue and gold of the more recent church.

Father Nicholas Coccola, who had succeeded Father Fouquet in the Kootenays, later succeeded Father Morice in the Babine district, and here in 1908 he built St. Mary Magdalen, replacing an earlier church. Coccola decorated the edifice with a dazzling sunburst window and numerous small spires and crosses, and although the interior has been modernized, the church remains a fine example of decorative native folk architecture.

For many years, the villages of the Upper Skeena west of Hagwilget remained the sole concern of the Methodists and the Church of England. The Protestant missionaries

St. Joseph's Mission, near Williams Lake (PABC)

often visited the area from their main stations on the coast of Fort Simpson, Kincolith and Metlakatla, but few permanent posts were established until the arrival of Mr. A.E. Price in Kitwanga in 1869. Others followed: Rev. Robert Tomlinson to Kispiox, Rev. W.H. Collison to Hazelton (Gitenmaks) and William Henry Pierce to Kitseguecla.

Pierce was born to a Tsimshian mother and a Scots apprentice serving the Hudson's Bay Company. After his mother's early death, he moved to Fort Simpson to live with his maternal grandfather. There he studied under the Anglican William Duncan and later, having met the Methodist Thomas Crosby in Victoria, returned to Fort Simpson to serve under him. Pierce was one of a kind — an Indian convert who could accomplish great work among his native followers. In 1877 he erected the Methodist Church at Port Essington, at the mouth of the Skeena, having convinced the villagers to travel forty-five miles in their canoes for the necessary lumber.

Eight years later Pierce and Crosby journeyed up the

Skeena, visiting Kitwanga, Kitwancool, Kispiox and Kitseguecla. Of his first visit to Kitseguecla, Pierce wrote in his book *From Potlatch to Pulpit,*

Here the whole tribe was engaged in potlatching and dancing.

As soon as we landed we held a service in front of the village and while singing, a dog-eater rushed out and threw a dead dog right in our midst, some of the blood splashing on our clothes.

St. Paul's, Kitwanga. Photo by C.F. Newcombe (BCPM)

Unintimidated, he stayed on in the village, living among the people and their great houses and totem poles, eventually erecting a mission church and school. He later moved to Kispiox, where he built a sawmill to aid the local economy and to provide the lumber for a new church in the village. Today a later building dedicated to Pierce stands in Kispiox. Ministered by the United Church, its unique and aging stepped tower honours the man who brought Christianity to much of the Skeena and who was a devoted servant to members of his race until his death in 1948.

In a 1911 photograph taken at Kitwanga by the ethnologist C.F. Newcombe, mission buildings can be seen standing among the houses, poles and mortuary boxes of this "place of the rabbits" on the Skeena. St. Paul's, built in 1893 by Rev. Alfred Price to replace an earlier church, still serves the village. Price came to Kitwanga in 1889 and set about learning the native language, translating his prayer books into the Gitksan tongue. He was aided in his work by Rev.

Robert Tomlinson, one of the great missionaries of the district, who at various times served on the Nass River, at Kispiox, and with Duncan at Metlakatla.

In 1887 Price resigned from the Church Missionary Society, wintered at Kitwanga, and the next year, taking converts with him, established a non-sectarian Christian village at Minskinish, fourteen miles downriver. Located on the west bank, it was a carefully planned and strictly governed mission. Price, like Pierce, built a sawmill—located across the river where the cable ferry now runs—and lumber cut there, spruce and cedar, was used in the construction of the Anglican church buildings at Kitwanga, Hazelton and Minskinish itself. Today at Minskinish—Cedarvale, as it is now called—only scant traces remain of the once-flourishing mission station. Cedars line the bank at the ferry landing, and solitary empty buildings weather in the now uncultivated fields.

†

On 23 December 1856, William Duncan, lay minister, recently of Beverley, England, carrying twenty-eight pieces of luggage, boarded H.M.S. *Satellite* bound for the Horn, Victoria and the land of the "savage tribes" of the Northwest Coast. An ardent disciple of the Anglican Church Missionary Society, Duncan established the first model village on the Pacific and became the most legendary and controversial missionary in the new Colony of British Columbia. Born of working-class parents, Duncan was self-educated and in everything he undertook was captivated by the Victorian ideal of moral and personal excellence. He grew up in an era of unprecedented change in England, brought about by the Industrial Revolution, urbanization and public reforms. New housing estates were devised for the workers, a great exhibition was held by Prince Albert in 1851, displaying the industry and goods of Great Britain and her Empire, and Englishmen rose to the challenge of civilizing primitive societies which they were certain were less fortunate than they. In this climate, and through the C.M.S. and its spokesman Henry Venn, Duncan learned of Evangelical Protestantism. By the age of twenty-four, he was ready to carry the gospel of the church to the heathen of the world, be it Africa, New Zealand, China or British Columbia. In fact he expected a posting in Africa but was sent instead to Fort Simpson, the centre of the Pacific fur trade and the gathering place of over two thousand Coast Tsimshians.

Duncan found that Indian attitudes of co-operation and competition suited his purposes—for communal support, self-government and work were paramount, in his view, to improving Indian life. After four years among the tribes of

KISPIOX UNITED CHURCH

CEDARVALE (MINSKINISH)

KITSEGUECLA

157

Fort Simpson, witnessing the degenerative influences of the white traders, he was able to convince fifty villagers to move with him to an old village site, Metlakatla, "the passage between two bodies of water," close to modern Prince Rupert. Duncan was careful to ensure that the Tsimshians initiated the move and selected the site. In this way, he encouraged a kind of native self-determination that was to bind the Metlakatlans together until 1887 when, challenged by the Church of England, he moved his model village to Alaska, never to return.

Duncan was a remarkable man; at first counsellor, preacher and educator, he soon became architect, manufacturer, bookkeeper, and magistrate, dealing justice to wayward whiskey traders who threatened his community. Temperance, order and prosperity reigned, and new converts joined the community every year. By the late 1870s, Bishop Hills, visiting the station, was able to write:

The new settlement has now grown to one thousand people, forming the healthiest and strongest settlement on the coast. Rules have been laid down for the regulation of the community, to which all residents are obliged to conform, and the use of spirituous liquors strictly prohibited. All are required to keep the Sabbath, attend church, and send their children to school. Industrious habits are diligently encouraged, and the people educated as farmers, blacksmiths, carpenters, merchants, etc. They live in well-built cottages, and have a beautiful Gothic church capable of seating one thousand persons. It is modelled after the old English cathedral, and was built by the Indian mechanics of that village. The average winter attendance is six hundred to eight hundred. They have also a school building that will accommodate seven hundred pupils. Besides these they have carpenter and blacksmith shops, storehouse, saw-mill, etc., all owned and managed by the Indians; while all around the bay are well cultivated gardens and potato patches. The main street of the village along the beach is lighted with street lamps. The population of 1,000 is divided into ten companies or wards, each having its elder to look after its religious services, its chief as leader in social gatherings, and one or two constables. The village has a brass band of twenty-four instruments, a public reading-room and public guest-house for the lodging of strange Indians. Fifty two-storey dwelling houses were in process of erection at the time of my visit....

As a missionary builder, Duncan was unequalled. Not only did he conceive of a town plan which spread out like wings from the centre hub containing a great wooden church and community building, he designed houses which were modelled after Victorian workers' dwellings and yet adapted to the special communal family needs of the natives. The first frame residences, 18' x 34', had multi-family apartments at each end of a central common room. Later, as the villagers became more autonomous, two-storey single-family units were linked together by a one-storey common area. The culminating structure, at Mission Point, was the Church of St. Paul's, constructed in 1874 with lumber from the village sawmill. It was a curious Gothic structure with a massive timber frame, shiplap planks and gingerbread trim. Consistent with Duncan's concern that no object or ritual be allowed to incite the emotions of the Indian people, his church was devoid of all crosses, altars and vestments, and he refused to offer Holy Communion. This and other autocratic actions led to his dismissal from the C.M.S. in 1881, after thirty years of service.

Bishop William Ridley, who had been appointed to take over the new Diocese of Caledonia found "an unexpected absence of Christian instruction and privileges in the settlement." Duncan and over six hundred Tsimshians moved seventy miles north, out of Ridley's territory, to Annette Island, Alaska, and there built New Metlakatla. For many years Bishop Ridley tended those remaining at the old village and the surrounding coastal missions, some of which were established under his direction. In 1901 a disastrous fire destroyed Metlakatla, including the great church and the Bishop's house containing his writings, anthropological collection and extensive library.

In the village today, the visitor finds little evidence of those romantic and prolific times. A grave monument and firebell sit close to where the old flag tower once stood, and poplar trees planted by Duncan line the road. In the church army hall, an ancient drum recalls the days when the brass band welcomed all visitors with a rousing rendition of "God Save the Queen." Victorian porcelain ware, brought from England by the Ridleys, can be seen in the new museum. Wild grass, fireweed, Indian rhubarb and salmonberry have taken over the garden plots. At the water's edge, where great canoes once rested, an abandoned jailhouse stands as a stern reminder of another era, but the land itself is as Duncan lovingly described it: "A rich verdure, a waving forest, backed by lofty, but densely-wooded mountains. A solemn stillness, broken only by the cries of flocks of happy birds...."

Fifteen miles north of the remains of Metlakatla sits the thriving community of Port Simpson. Once the site of the most important Hudson's Bay Company trading post on the North Coast—and then called Fort rather than Port Simpson—it was also the location of Rev. Thomas Crosby's renowned Methodist Christian village. Today the Indian Brotherhood Cannery dominates the town, but two wooden churches and a band shelter are left as reminders

Duncan's Church of St. Paul at Metlakatla (PABC)

Interior of the church at Metlakatla (PABC)

of those days when "the Blessed Spirit came down in great power upon the people."

Crosby, who began his lifelong work in British Columbia in 1862, spent his first ten years on Vancouver Island and at Chilliwack. In 1873, he journeyed to Ontario to marry and raise mission funds, and a year later returned to minister for over twenty years to the Tsimshian, Haida and Bella Coola tribes. He and his bride arrived at Fort Simpson by canoe, alighting

in front of the old Hudson's Bay Company fort, and there shook hands with hundreds of people, some fairly well dressed, some in meagre clothing, others rigged out in gay-coloured blankets and shawls, and some with painted faces.

Crosby soon convinced the Indians to form a municipal council, build new houses, lay out a grid of streets and erect a bridge to the old reserve site on Village Island. In two years, sixty separate homes surrounded a prominent church on the hillside. Crosby had brought along plans, prepared by architect-contractor Thomas Trounce of Victoria, for a building which seated one thousand people. It measured 50' x 80' and was "Gothic in style with buttresses and a tower 140 feet high." The church was built to these heroic proportions by the villagers themselves, who not only supplied the material and labour required but also helped raise the funds, giving generously of their treasured blankets, furs, muskets and silver jewellery.

Rev. Crosby, through his Council of Chiefs and their watchmen, ruled the settlement with an iron hand. Laws were enacted "allowing no Sabbath-breaking, no dog-eating, no whiskey-drinking . . . and no heathen marriages." Gambling was forbidden, and the rattling or "demon work" of the shaman was outlawed. Those who violated the rules served out their punishment by building roads and bridges. Industrial fairs were held and prizes given for carving, furniture making, and for the best-built house or boat, or best-kept garden. A brass band and a fire company were formed, a rifle company organized, and a little paper was published: the *Simpson Herald*.

Emma Crosby established the first home for Indian girls in the village, and soon afterward a boarding house for boys was erected. Many of the students became teachers and workers in the mission field, accelerating Rev. Crosby's influence. With his beloved 21-foot steam launch *The Glad Tidings*, he conveyed evangelistic workers and carried lumber to build churches, schools and improve native villages. In her heyday, this floating mission covered nine thousand miles a year, carrying the gospel to every tribe and mining, logging and fishing camp on the coast. In 1897 Crosby was still hard at it:

PORT SIMPSON METHODIST CHURCH
Opposite: METLAKATLA

From the commencement of the mission at Port Simpson in 1874, there have been built in the District over thirty churches, or preaching places; one girl's home; one boarding school for boys... and three hospitals. About fifteen hundred church members have been gathered in and we are reaching some ten thousand people with gospel light. ... Hence, as our friends will see, the good ship The Glad Tidings *is much needed yet to reach all the inlets and bays where the regular steamers do not go. We have had her repaired... and we do hope our friends will come to our help to pay the bills.*

As Metlakatla flourished, and before Thomas Crosby's arrival on the North Coast, a new Anglican mission was established on the Nass River, directed towards the conversion of the Niskas, or the Nass people. In 1864 Rev. R.A. Doolan erected a mission house twenty miles from the mouth of the river at Abanshekgues. Three years later, he and Rev. Robert Tomlinson floated the log building downstream on a raft to Kincolith, "the place of scalps."

Tomlinson's intention was to start a model village patterned after Metlakatla. Close to the mission house, he constructed a log church—divided into a schoolroom and an eighty-seat chapel—as well as a trading store and an eleven-bed hospital. The good Reverend had received thorough medical training in Dublin, and his reputation as a skilled doctor extended throughout the entire district. Through medical treatment and education, he was able to expose the unbelievers to the "glorious and precious truths of the Gospel."

In 1883 one of the North Coast's outstanding missionaries, Rev. William H. Collison, who had been assisting the Skeena missions, came to Kincolith, where his Christian Indian followers erected new dwellings and a larger church. Housing was laid out in neat rows from a central church position. Although the houses were separated to prevent the spread of fire, half the village, including Collison's church, was destroyed in 1893.

The burning shingles were lifted by the wind, which was blowing strongly from the west, and were landed on the roofs of the church and other buildings, a quarter of a mile distant. Every such burning brand kindled fresh flames against which the fire fighters had but slight chances of success.

A new church was quickly erected with funds received from the chiefs, villagers, and friends from England. This new Christ Church dominates Kincolith today, its twin spires and nave sharp and white against the forest's misty green.

Two and one-half miles below Gitlakdamiks on the

McCullagh's Holy Trinity Church, Aiyansh (PABC)

upper Nass stands the wooden remnant of Rev. James B. McCullagh's model village, Old Aiyansh. Established in 1877, the Christian village grew and flourished until destroyed by a great November flood forty years later. McCullagh, by tireless work against great odds, had built a sawmill, a school, a mission house and one of the finest Gothic churches in the Church Missionary Society's domain. Bishop Ridley, visiting Aiyansh in 1895, commented on McCullagh's architectural skills:

On the east side of the church stands one of the prettiest schoolhouses I have seen. The interior arrangements and exterior decorations of all these new buildings, private and public, expressed the ideas of a single mind. It is a model village, planned by an artist's eye and pleasing in every feature.

McCullagh himself recounted the building of the church, which he named Holy Trinity:

Oh the joy of building this sanctuary in the wild forest! For days at a time we were up to our armpits in the cold water of some mountain stream, removing obstructions and taking out logs, yet nobody caught cold and there were no complaints.... We managed to complete the frame and roof in the chancel before the winter.... In May we resumed operations, the most difficult part of our task being the dressing and setting up of the large cedar cross-beams forming the interior of the roof.... I reserved work on the chancel for myself alone, carving two large cross-beams over the screen and otherwise attempting to beautify the interior.

Holy Trinity boasted the only round spire in British Columbia, 106 feet high. Its interior was finished in yellow balsam, red cedar and spruce. In 1919, after the flood, McCullagh witnessed the relocation and reconstruction of his cathedral as Church Army Hall in Gitlakdamiks. His great desire was fulfilled: "the villages became one and the people one — no longer two, but one people."

From the Queen Charlotte Islands the Haida came to Metlakatla to trade, and Duncan's work attracted much interest among them. They in their turn caught the attention of Rev. Collison, who was already at work among the Tsimshian in the early 1870s.

Concerned that the Church Missionary Society had established two missions at Metlakatla and Kincolith serving one linguistic group, Collison sought and received permission to move among the Haida at Masset. Boldly setting out in a war canoe with a Tsimshian crew, he crossed Dixon's Entrance, a hundred-mile journey over dangerous open water. He was to make the trip often, starting out from the mainland across the wind-swept sea, past the white sand bar of Rose Spit and into Masset Sound to the villages of Masset and Yan. Here in 1876, among the great houses and poles of this prolific and powerful village, he established a mission and, aided by his wife, ministered to the heathen — first in an abandoned longhouse and later in a commodious Gothic church erected by his associate, Rev. Charles Harrison.

In the modern village of Masset, a new St. John the Evangelist, constructed in 1922, has replaced the old. Close by stands a bear totem recently carved by Robert Davidson, Jr., grandson of the chief of the abandoned village of Yan, and one of the outstanding young carvers working again in the traditional styles. The pole was raised by the villagers in August 1969, in a land from which nearly all the old monuments had been removed to museums or had rotted into the ground. But across the channel the Great Eagle of Yan still stands, a proud remnant of a culture unequalled on the North Pacific Coast.

†

Sacred places have always been found in the natural landscape, and one of the most beautiful of all is the lush hillside amphitheatre called Botanie, which lies from Masset nearly a thousand miles back along the road so often travelled by the missionaries, traders, gold seekers and church builders whose legacy is the subject of this book. Here, just above Lytton, in 1884, in a valley filled with summer wildflowers, over nine hundred devout Indian converts gathered to participate in the religious ceremony conducted by the Anglican Bishop Acton Sillitoe. They came from all directions across the pine-covered slopes of the Thompson and Fraser rivers. "Large numbers had responded to my call," Sillitoe said,

and a great opportunity was before us. A flag floated over nearly every tent, in most instances the diocesan flag, blue with gold cross and mitre; and the whole scene was bright....

As their horses watered at the mountain stream near the encampment, the Indians gathered edible roots which flourished on the slopes. Lectures, services and celebrations were held, and there were many baptisms. Bishop Sillitoe dealt at one meeting with errant medicine men, lumping these with "whiskey and gambling" cases, and then offered a potlatch, distributing knives, fishhooks, pictures and tobacco.

Over the days of worship and confessions, communion was celebrated at a rough altar set under a baldachin of wildflowers on a platform covered with pine branches. At nightfall, campfires were lit and "cooking, feasting, smoking, chatting, singing, or rest, pure and simple, varied the aspect of each group of tents."

This great gathering was remembered long after Bishop Sillitoe's death in 1894. And it is possible today to journey to the valley of the Botanie — to imagine there the pageantry of a century ago, and amid the delicacy and colour of its meadows in full bloom, to seek the silence and the sacredness of the place once more.

THE GREAT EAGLE OF YAN

BOTANIE VALLEY

SKEDANS

LYTTON

FRIENDLY COVE: MEMORIAL ERECTED 1902–3 AT THE DEATH OF CHIEF MAQUINNA (PHOTO BY C.H. FRENCH: BCPM)

NORTH VANCOUVER: ST. PAUL'S

Glossary of Architectural Terms

ARCADE   A series of arches—two at least—forming a single architectural feature.

AUREOLA   A halo, or its sculptural or pictorial representation in an architectural setting.

BALDACHIN   A canopy, usually of rich cloth, and especially one suspended over an altar.

BELL-CAST ROOF   A pitched roof which curves outwards at its lower edges like a bell.

BELL COT   A bell house: the roofed structure, usually built on the roof, which shelters and carries the church's bell or bells (also often spelled *bell cote*).

BUTTRESS   A projecting structure or pier which strengthens a wall or counteracts its outward thrust. A false buttress, of course, is one which, intentionally, does no real strengthening and has no structural function.

CHANCEL   The portion of the church set apart for the clergy and containing the altar.

CLAPBOARD   [pronounced *klab*urd]   Siding of horizontal wooden boards, usually cut thicker at one edge than at the other and each overlapping the one below to produce a weatherproof surface.

CLOCHER   A bell tower, steeple or roof structure including bellmount and bells, and usually capped with a spire or flèche.

CORBEL   A bracket—usually made by extending successive courses of masonry or a structure of wood from the wall surface—used to support a vault rib, beam, or other structural member.

CORNICE   A decorative projection crowning the top of a wall or supporting the edge of a roof.

CRENELATED   Notched so as to simulate battlements. (The solids or teeth of the battlements are called merlons, and the intervening notches or voids are called crenels.)

CROCKET   A projecting piece of sculpture, usually at the edge of a gable or spire, or on a reredos, often carved as a piece of leafage.

DORMER   A projection from a pitched roof, often containing a window.

FINIAL   A culminating ornament at the top of a spire or other structure.

FLÈCHE   A particularly slender spire, usually forming part of the roof structure.

FLUTE   A decorative groove or channel.

GABLE   The triangular piece of wall enclosing the end of a pitched roof.

GABLET   A miniature gable, often used as decoration.

HAMMER BEAM   A short beam projecting from a wall and supporting one end of an arch or roof timber.

ITALIANATE   In architecture, this term is applied to buildings descended from the vernacular farmhouse architecture of the Italian countryside. Symptoms of the style are asymmetry; towers or cupolas; low-pitched, bracketed roofs or cornices, and round-headed windows.

LANTERN   A structure which rises above the roof and,

through openings in its sides, lights the interior of the building.

LICH GATE   A covered gate at the entrance to a cemetery.

NAVE   That part of a church in which the congregation is seated.

NIMBUS   A halo, especially a simple, circular one.

PALISADE   A barrier composed of long stakes driven into the earth one adjacent the other.

PINNACLE   A turret or small spire rising from the roof or other base structure.

QUATREFOIL   A circular or arched form with four lobes.

RENAISSANCE REVIVAL   In architecture, a style involving symmetrical elevations crowned with bold, elaborate cornices, and often the superimposition onto the wall surface of columns and entablatures of one or more of the classic orders.

REREDOS   An ornamental screen or wall at the back of an altar.

ROMANESQUE   A style of architecture based on Roman imperial design, marked by rounded arches and by heavy rustication emphasizing lintels, arches and other structural elements.

ROSE WINDOW   A circular window filled with decorative tracery radiating from its centre.

RUSTICATION   The deliberate use of rough-cut stone or wood to achieve a weathered or rustic appearance.

SANCTUARY   Chancel.

SCISSOR TRUSS   A roof truss in which the feet of the principal rafters are each connected to the upper half of the opposite rafter by ties which cross, like open scissors, in the middle. A triangular truss, in other words, in which the bottom rib of the triangle is removed and replaced by two intersecting cross-ties, which angle upward less steeply than the roof itself.

TABERNACLE   A recess, usually decorated, for holding consecrated objects.

TREFOIL   A circular or arched form with three lobes.

TUSCAN   An architectural style or mode marked by straight-fronted, symmetrical buildings, often capped with massive cornices. Rusticated quoins (corner stones) are another distinguishing feature, and the base storey wall is sometimes also heavily textured. (Also called *Romano-Tuscan*.)

VERNACULAR   The architectural style native to the place.

VESTRY   A room adjoining the chancel or choir of a church, used for the storage of sacred objects.

Suggestions for Further Reading

GENERAL STUDIES (ARCHITECTURE)

GOWANS, ALAN. *Building Canada.* Oxford University Press, Toronto, 1966.

KALMAN, HAROLD, & JOHN DE VISSER. *Pioneer Churches.* McClelland & Stewart, Toronto, 1976.

PUGIN, A. WELBY. *The True Principles of Pointed or Christian Architecture.* Henry G. Bohn, London, 1853.

SEGGER, MARTIN, & DOUGLAS FRANKLIN. *Victoria: A Primer for Regional History in Architecture.* American Life Foundation & Study Institute, Watkins Glen, N.Y., 1979.

STANTON, PHOEBE B. *Pugin.* The Viking Press, New York, 1972.

VEILLETTE, JOHN, & GARY WHITE. *Early Indian Village Churches.* University of British Columbia Press, Vancouver, 1977.

GENERAL STUDIES (GEOGRAPHIC & HISTORICAL)

AKRIGG, G.P.V., & HELEN B. AKRIGG. *1001 British Columbia Place Names.* 3rd ed. Discovery Press, Vancouver, 1973.

BRYAN, LIZ, & JACK BRYAN. *Backwoods of British Columbia.* Sunflower Books, Vancouver, 1975.

CLARK, KENNETH. *The Gothic Revival.* Harper & Row, New York, 1961.

CRONIN, KAY. *Cross in the Wilderness.* Mitchell Press, Vancouver, 1960.

FISHER, ROBIN. *Contact and Conflict: Indian-European Relations in British Columbia, 1774-1890.* University of British Columbia Press, Vancouver, 1977.

HOWAY, F.W., & E.O.S. SCHOLEFIELD. *British Columbia.* 4 vols. S.J. Clarke, Vancouver, 1914.

HUTCHINSON, BRUCE. *The Fraser.* Rinehart & Co., New York, 1950.

LARGE, R.G. *The Skeena, River of Destiny.* Mitchell Press, Vancouver, 1957.

MORICE, REV. A.-G. *History of the Catholic Church in Western Canada.* 2 vols. Musson Book Co., Toronto, 1910.

———. *Fifty Years in Western Canada; Being the Abridged Memoirs of Rev. A.-G. Morice, O.M.I.* Ryerson Press, Toronto, 1930.

ORMSBY, MARGARET A. *British Columbia: A History.* Macmillan, Toronto, 1971.

PEAKE, FRANK A. *The Anglican Church in British Columbia.* Mitchell Press, Vancouver, 1959.

RAMSEY, BRUCE. *Ghost Towns of British Columbia.* Mitchell Press, Vancouver, 1970.

WALBRAN, JOHN T. *British Columbia Coast Names.* J.J. Douglas, Vancouver, 1971.

THOSE HERE BEFORE

BOAS, FRANZ. *Kwakiutl Ethnology.* Edited by Helen Codere. University of Chicago Press, Chicago, 1966.

DRUCKER, PHILIP. *Cultures of the North Pacific Coast.* Chandler Publishing, San Francisco, 1965.

DUFF, WILSON. *The Indian History of British Columbia, Vol. I: The Impact of the White Man.* Provincial Museum of Natural History & Anthropology, Victoria, 1969.

HARRISON, CHARLES. *Ancient Warriors of the North Pacific.* H.F. & G. Witherby, London, 1925.

TRADERS & MISSIONARIES

COOK, WARREN L. *Flood Tide of Empire: Spain and the Pacific Northwest, 1543-1819.* Yale University Press, New Haven, 1973.

DEMERS, FATHER MODESTE, & FATHER FRANÇOIS BLANCHET. *Notices and Voyages of the Famed Quebec Mission to the Pacific Northwest.* Champoeg Press, Reed College, Portland, for the Oregon Historical Society, 1956.

MORICE, REV. A.-G. *The History of the Northern Interior of British Columbia.* John Lane, The Bodley Head, London, 1906; reprinted by Ye Galleon Press, Fairfield, Wash., 1971.

MOZIÑO, JOSÉ MARIANO. *Noticias de Nutka: An Account of Nootka in 1792.* McClelland & Stewart, Toronto, 1970.

PETHICK, DEREK. *James Douglas: Servant of Two Empires.* Mitchell Press, Vancouver, 1969.

FAITH, SETTLEMENT & CHURCH BUILDING

COLUMBIA MISSION. *Annual Report,1860-1880/81.* Rivingtons, London, 1860-1881.

DAVIS, REV. E.A. *Commemorative Review of the Methodist Presbyterian & Congregational Churches in British Columbia.* Joseph Lee, Vancouver, 1925.

GREGSON, HARRY. *A History of Victoria, 1842-1970.* J.J. Douglas, Victoria, 1977.

HOWAY, F.W. *The Work of the Royal Engineers in British Columbia, 1858–1863.* Queen's Printer, Victoria, 1910.

WOODLAND, ALAN. *New Westminster: The Early Years, 1858-1898.* Nunaga Publishing, New Westminster, 1973.

GOLD TRAIL MISSIONS

LUDDITT, FRED W. *Barkerville Days.* Mitchell Press, Vancouver, 1969.

THE GREAT CONVERSION

COLLISON, REV. W.H. *In the Wake of the War Canoe.* Musson Book Co., Toronto, 1916.

CROSBY, REV. THOMAS. *Among the An-ko-me-nums.* William Briggs, Toronto, 1907.

———. *Up and Down the North Pacific Coast.* F.C. Stephenson, Methodist Mission Rooms, Toronto, 1914.

GOWEN, REV. HERBERT H. *Church Work in British Columbia; Being a Memoir of the Episcopate of Acton Windeyer Sillitoe, D.D., D.C.I., First Bishop of New Westminster.* Longmans, Green & Co., London, 1899.

JOHNSON, OLGA WEYDEMEYER. *Flathead and Kootenay: The Rivers, the Tribes and the Region's Traders.* Arthur H. Clark Co., Glendale, Calif., 1969.

MOSER, REV. CHARLES. *Reminiscences of the West Coast of Vancouver Island.* Acme Press, Victoria, 1926.

USHER, JEAN. *William Duncan of Metlakatla.* National Museums of Canada Publications in History, no. 5. Ottawa, 1974.

Index